1 MONTH OF
FREE
READING

at
www.ForgottenBooks.com

By purchasing this book you are eligible for one month membership to ForgottenBooks.com, giving you unlimited access to our entire collection of over 1,000,000 titles via our web site and mobile apps.

To claim your free month visit:
www.forgottenbooks.com/free190519

ISBN 978-0-484-59742-5
PIBN 10190519

TABLE OF CONTENTS.

371704

INTRODUCTORY.

The Handbook for the Noncommissioned Officer of Infantry is a compilation drawn in great part from the Army Regulations, Infantry Drill Regulations, Manual of Guard Duty, U. S. Army, "The Service of Security and Information" and "Organization and Tactics," by Colonel Arthur L. Wagner, Assistant Adjutant-General, U. S. Army.

Those chapters not drawn from either of these sources are merely outlines of the various duties which noncommissioned officers are called upon to perform, and which, in the absence of manuals, have been more or less traditional.

The Handbook is not designed to replace any of the above manuals, but to assist the noncommissioned officer in the study of all by placing before him in brief and compact order a comprehensive idea of the scope of his duties and responsibilities.

The various chapters cover all the duties which the noncommissioned officer of the line of infantry will ordinarily be called upon to perform, and the points touched upon are those most important and essential to the proper performance of those duties.

It is designed for use in the schools of the noncommissioned officer and for the study especially of newly appointed and inexperienced noncommissioned officers.

The author is indebted to the late Colonel Arthur L. Wagner, Assistant Adjutant-General, U. S. Army, for permission to use his works and plates on the subjects of "The Service of Security and Information" and "Organization and Tactics," both of which books have been extensively drawn upon; also to Major Chase W. Kennedy, Adjutant-General's Department, for many valuable suggestions and much valuable criticism.

CHAPTER I.

THE NONCOMMISSIONED OFFICER.

1. The noncommissioned officer is selected from the enlisted men of the company, for his character, intelligence, efficiency, and soldierly bearing, to assist the commissioned officer in the instruction, discipline, and care of the other enlisted men.

2. He holds his rank and exercises authority within certain limits by virtue of a warrant.

3. Noncommissioned officers will be carefully selected and instructed, and always supported by the company commanders in the proper performance of their duties. They will not be detailed for any duty or permitted to engage in any occupation inconsistent with their rank and position. Officers will be cautious in reproving them in the presence or hearing of private soldiers. A. R. 270.

4. Company noncommissioned officers are appointed by the regimental commander, or by the battalion commander under certain conditions, on the recommendation of their company commanders; but in no case will any company organization have an excess of noncommissioned officers above that allowed by law. A. R. 271.

5. The number of noncommissioned officers allowed by law for any company varies with the authorized strength of the company, and is announced from time to time in general orders. In general, however, the noncommissioned officers of a company of infantry consist of one first sergeant, one quartermaster sergeant, from four to six sergeants, and from six to ten corporals.

6. To test the capacity of privates for the duties of noncommissioned officers, company commanders may appoint lance-corporals, who will be obeyed and respected as corporals, but no company shall have more than one lance-corporal at a time, unless

there are non-commissioned officers absent by authority, during which absences there may be one for each absentee.

7. Each noncommissioned officer will be furnished with a warrant or certificate of his rank, signed by the officer making the appointment, and countersigned by the adjutant; but a separate warrant as first sergeant, quartermaster sergeant, or stable sergeant will not be given. A warrant issued to a noncommissioned officer is his personal property. Warrants need not be renewed in cases of re-enlistment in the same company, if re-enlistment is made the day following the day of discharge, but, upon request, may remain in force until vacated by promotion or reduction, each re-enlistment and continuance to be noted on the warrant by the company commander. A. R. 274.

9. The captain will select the first sergeant from the sergeants of his company, and may return him to the grade of sergeant without reference to higher authority. A. R. 273.

10. Appointments of company noncommissioned officers will take effect on the day of appointment by the authorized commander, and of first sergeants, quartermaster sergeants, stable sergeants, . . . on the day of appointment by the company commander; but in case of vacancy in a company in the field and absent from regimental headquarters, a company commander may make a temporary appointment of a noncommissioned officer, which, if approved by the regimental commander, will carry rank and pay from date of such appointment. A. R. 275.

11. A noncommissioned officer may be reduced to the ranks by sentence of a court-martial, or on the recommendation of the company commander, by the order of the commander having authority to appoint such noncommissioned officer, but a noncommissioned officer will not be reduced because of absence on account of sickness, or injury contracted in line of duty. If reduced to the ranks by sentence of a court-martial at a post not the headquarters of his regiment, the company commander will forward a transcript

f the order to the regimental commander. The desertion of a non-ommissioned officer vacates his position on the date of desertion. ι. R. 276.

12. The detail of a noncommissioned officer on extra duty, ther than that of overseer, will not be made, except in cases of mergency, without prior approval of the department commander. ι noncommissioned officer will not be detailed on any duty incon-istent with his rank and position in the military service. A. R. 271.

13. The noncommissioned officer should, by his military earing, dignified conduct, and strict compliance with all orders nd regulations, set an example to the other enlisted men. He hould, by study of the service books and manuals, thoroughly ac-uaint himself with the extent and character of his duties and re-ponsibilities, in order that he may instruct those under him in an fficient and intelligent manner. He should, in addition, acquire a horough knowledge of the details of all duties required of those nder his command or instruction. After becoming proficient in is own duties, he should acquire some knowledge of the duties of he next higher grade, as he may be called on to perform them in he absence of his seniors.

14. In the exercise of command, he should be firm, dignified, nd patient, without harshness or unnecessary display of authority. ιy a careful and quiet use of his authority and influence, he should ndeavor to prevent the occurrence of anything which would tend ɔ promote discontent or lack of harmonious feelings in the company.

15. It is the duty of the noncommissioned officers at all times nd under all circumstances, whether on or off duty, in or out of the ost, to check promptly all disputes, quarrels, or disorderly conduct mong enlisted men which would lead to an infraction of orders or ιgulations, or would tend to bring disrepute upon the service.

16. Noncommissioned officers against whom charges may be teferred for trial will be placed in arrest in their barracks or quar-ιrs. They will not be confined in the guard-house in company with rivates, except in aggravated cases or where escape is feared.

17. Noncommissioned officers in arrest will not be required to perform any duty in which they may be called upon to exercise any command. Noncommissioned officers in confinement will not be sent out to work with prisoners under sentence.

18. Noncommissioned officers will not, if they object thereto, be brought to trial before a regimental garrison, or summary court-martial, without the authority of the officer competent to order their trial by general court-martial. . . . . A. R. 958.

19. A noncommissioned officer in command of a company, after aligning it at the formation of the battalion, takes post on the right of the right guide; he takes the post of the captain when the battalion is in column. At parade, before bringing the company to parade rest, he comes to the trail, steps two paces to the front and faces to the left, retaining the piece at the trail; having given his commands, he resumes his post and comes to parade rest.

20. In exercises in the manual, noncommisssoned officers commanding companies or subdivisions execute only the order and parade rest; in rendering honors, they present; while marching, they carry their pieces in the same same position as the men.

21. When a noncommissioned officer, while in arrest or confinement, is reduced by sentence of a court-martial, the date of the order publishing the sentence is the date of reduction. In all other cases reduction takes effect on the date of receipt of the order at the soldier's station.

22. When passing in review, a non-commissioned officer commanding a company or platoon executes the rifle salute; when commanding a company or detachment separate from a battalion or other command, on passing the colors or any person entitled to the compliment, he salutes in the same manner, first bringing his command to the *eyes right* (or *left*).

CHAPTER II.

THE NONCOMMISSIONED OFFICER AS INSTRUCTOR.

23.   In the school of the soldier, the sergeants and corporals are generally the instructors, under the supervision of a commissioned officer.

24.   In all drills, and especially in those of recruits in the school of the soldier, short and frequent drills are preferable to long ones, which exhaust the attention of both instructor and men.

25.   The instructor should, by careful study and practice, make himself thoroughly familiar with the details of every movement which he desires the recruit to execute. He should, before each drill, read over that portion of the Drill Regulations which pertains to the drill or instruction of the day.

26.   The instructor will always maintain a military bearing, and by a quiet, firm demeanor, set a proper example to the men.

27.   The instructor explains the movement to be executed in as few words as possible, at the same time executing it himself.   In explaining the movements, the instructor should be careful to do so in language which the recruit will understand; and when it becomes necessary to use technical expressions, he should explain them fully and ascertain by questioning if their meaning is understood by the men under instruction.

28.   He requires the recruits to take by themselves the proper positions, and does not touch them for the purpose of correcting them, except when they are unable to correct themselves; he avoids keeping them too long at the same movement, although each should be understood before passing to another. He exacts by degrees the desired precision and uniformity.

29.   After the movements have been properly executed in the order laid down, he no longer confines himself to that order.

30. When the execution of a movement is improperly begun, and the instructor wishes to begin it anew for the purpose of correcting it, he commands, *As you were*, at which the movement ceases and the former position is resumed. To stay the execution of a movement when marching for the correction of errors the instructor commands: 1. *In place*, 2. *Halt*, when all halt and stand fast. To resume the movement he commands: 1. *Resume*, 2. *March*.

31. The instructor should exercise great care in the giving of commands. The tone of the commands should be animated, distinct, and of a loudness proportioned to the strength of the command under instruction.

32. Military commands are of two kinds. The preparatory command, such as, *Forward* or *Right shoulder*, indicates the movement which is to be executed. The command of execution, such as, *March*, *Halt*, or *Arms*, causes the execution of the movement.

33. The preparatory command should be given at such an interval of time before the command of execution as to admit of its being properly understood; the command of execution should be given at the instant that the movement is to commence.

34. Each preparatory command is pronounced in an ascending tone of voice, but always in such a manner that the command of execution may be given in a more elevated and energetic tone.

35. The command of execution should be pronounced in a firm and brief tone.

36. The proper giving of commands is of the utmost importance in securing uniformity and precision in the execution of all movements.

37. In the different schools, the posts of the noncommissioned officers are specified, but, when acting as instructors, they may go wherever their presence is necessary, or wherever they may best observe the execution of the movements.

CHAPTER III.

THE NONCOMMISSIONED OFFICER AS GUIDE.

38. A guide is an officer, noncommissioned officer, or private, upon whom the command, or fraction thereof, regulates its march.

39. The guide should always bear in mind that the precise execution of all movements by the company depends on the accurate and faithful performance of duty on the part of the guide. The dress and alignment of a company in line cannot be preserved unless the guide preserves a uniform cadence in marching and directs his march in a straight line. In column of fours of squads the dress and marching of the squads is equally dependent upon the action of the guide.

40. They should bear in mind that in order to direct the line of march in any direction, it is necessary to select *two* points on the line in their front and so direct their march as to keep these two points covered while advancing. They should exercise themselves in thus marching whenever opportunity offers itself.

41. The positions of the guides of a company in line are as follows: The right guide is in the front rank on the right of the first platoon; he is the right guide of this platoon and also of the company. The left guide is in the front rank on the left of the second platoon; he is the left guide of this platoon and also of the company. The left guide of the first platoon is in the line of file-closers, in rear of the second file from the left of the first platoon. The right guide of the second platoon is in the line of file-closers, in rear of the second file from the right of the second platoon. In platoon formations the left guide of the first platoon and the right guide of the second platoon take their positions in the front rank on the left and right of their respective platoons.

42. In column of squads and twos, the leading and rear guides

are in front and rear, respectively, of the leading or rear file on the side opposite the file-closers. Those guides already in the file-closers conform to the movements of the file-closers.

43. The point of rest is the point at which any formation begins.

44. Successive formations include formations, either into line or column, in which the several subdivisions arrive in their places successively—that is, one after the other.

45. In all successive formations into line, the guides of the company first to arrive are posted on the line, opposite the right and left files of the company and facing toward the point of rest. These guides are posted by either the adjutant or sergeant-major, according to which is nearest the head of the column or the point of rest.

46. In formations from a halt, the guides are posted at the preparatory command indicating the direction in which the line is to extend; if marching, they hasten toward their positions at the preparatory command, and are posted at the command *March.*

47. In the formations on right (left) into line from column of companies, the first guide is posted eight paces to the right (left) of the leading company. When executed from column of squads, the guides are posted eight paces from the right (left) flank of the leading company excluding the file-closers; the guide at the point of rest being posted opposite the front rank of the rear squad. This distance of eight paces may be increased when desired.

48. In the formations front into line from column of companies, the guides are posted against the leading company. When executed from column of squads, the guide at the point of rest is posted five paces to the front and five paces to the right or left of the front rank of the leading squad of the leading company. This distance of five paces may be increased when desired.

49. In the deployments, the guides are posted against the leading company.

50. The line is prolonged as in forming the battalion; the guides are assured by the adjutant or sergeant-major nearest the point of rest, or by both if the formation be central.

51. Companies are halted one pace from the line of guides, and immediately dressed up to them toward the point of rest.

52. When the principles of successive formations are well understood by the guides, they may be required to post themselves.

53. The major commands: 1. *Guides*, 2. *Posts*, at the completion of all successive formations into line.

54. In successive formations, should the major desire to commence firing pending the completion of the movement, he instructs the captains as to the kind of fire; the adjutant or sergeant at the head of the column cautions the guides not to take post marking the line.

55. After a company has moved up to its guides at the command *Dress*, the file opposite the guide nearest the point of rest stands fast and the company is not moved to the right or left for the correction of an error of interval unless the major so directs.

56. When a company in line is advancing toward the line of guides, the front rank man on the indicated flank acts as guide and directs his march on the guide of his company posted nearest the point of rest.

57. In forming the battalion, the center company is conducted by its captain so as to arrive from the rear, parallel to the line; its right and left guides precede it on the line by about twenty paces, taking post facing to the left (point of rest) at order arms, so that their elbows are against the breasts of the right and left files of the base company when it is dressed; they are posted under the direction of the adjutant and sergeant-major.

58. The line of guides is prolonged to the right by the right and left guides of companies of the right wing who precede their companies on the line by about twenty paces, and establish themselves facing toward the point of rest so that each is opposite the proper

flank of his company when it is on the line; the left guide places himself about five paces from the right guide of the preceding company.   The adjutant aligns the guides, placing himself in rear of the right guides of companies as they successively arrive.

The line of guides is similarly prolonged to the left by the guides of companies of the left wing, the sergeant-major aligning them in their positions, placing himself successively in rear of the left guides.

59.   Guides in front marking the line, in alignments and in successive formations, including the formation of the battalion, stand at the order.

60.   In all changes by squads from line into column, column into line, or from column of squads to twos, files, or the reverse, and in all turns about by squads, either in line or column, the guides and file-closers take their proper places in the most convenient way as soon as practicable after the command *March.*

61.   Marching in Line, to Effect a Slight Change of Direction. The captain commands: *Incline to the right (left).*   The guide gradually advances the left shoulder and marches in the new direction; all the files advance the left shoulder and conform to the movements of the guide, lengthening or shortening the step, according as the change is toward the side of the guide, or the side opposite.

62.   Guides and enlisted men in the line of file-closers execute the manual of arms during the drill unless specially excused, when they remain at the order.   During ceremonies they execute all movements.

A noncommissioned officer as guide, or in command of a company, sub-division, or detachment, carries his piece as the men do.

63.   Being in line; to turn on the fixed pivot, the captain commands: 1. *Company right (left)*,   2. *March;*   3. *Company,*   4. *Halt;* or,   3. *Forward,*   4. *March.*

At the second command, the right-flank man in the front rank faces to the right in marching and marks time; the other front-rank men oblique to the right, place themselves abreast of the pivot, and mark time; in the rear rank the third man from the right, followed in column by the second and first, moves straight to the front until in rear of his front-rank man, when all face to the right in marching and mark time; the remaining men of the rear rank move straight to the front four paces, oblique to the right, place themselves abreast of the third man, cover their file leaders, and mark time; the right guide steps back, takes post on the flank, and marks time.

The fourth command is given when the last man is one pace in rear of the new line.

The command *Halt* may be given at any time after the movement begins; only those halt who are in the new position. Each of the others halts upon arriving on the line, aligns himself to the right, and executes *front* without command.

64. Being in line; to turn on the moving pivot, the captain commands: 1. *Right (left) turn*, 2. *March;* 3. *Forward*, 4. *March.*

At the second command, the right-flank man faces to the right in marching and takes the half step; the other front-rank men oblique to the right until opposite their places in line, execute a second right oblique and take the half step when abreast of the right-flank man; the rear rank advances and turns on the same ground and in the same manner as the front rank, maintaining the distance of forty inches. All take the full step at the fourth command, which is given when the last man arrives in his new position.

Being at a halt, the movement is executed by the same commands and in the same manner. At the second command, the right flank man faces to the right as in marching and steps off, at half step.

Right (Left) half turn is executed in a similar manner. The right-flank man makes a half change of direction to the right and the other men make quarter changes in obliquing.

65. To give the battalion a new alignment: 1. *Guides center (right or left) company on the line*, 2. *Guides on the line*, 3. *Center (right or left)*, 4. *Dress*, 5. *Guides*, 6. *Posts.*

At the first command, the designated guides place themselves on the line facing the center (right or left); the major establishes them in the direction he wishes to give the battalion.

At the second command, the guides of the other companies take the same posts as in forming the battalion.

At the command *Dress*, each captain dresses his company to the flank toward which the guides face.

At the command *Posts*, the guides return to their posts.

66. In opening ranks of the company, the front rank executes right dress; the rear rank and the file-closers march backwards four steps, halt, and execute right dress; the lieutenants pass around their respective flanks and take post, facing to the front, three paces in front of the center of their respective platoons. The captain aligns the front rank, rear rank, and file-closers, takes post three paces in front of the right guide, facing to the left, and commands: *Front.*

67. In all changes of squads from line into column or from column into line, or from column of squads to twos, files, or the reverse, and in all wheel about by squads, either in line or column, the guides take their proper places in the most convenient way as soon as practicable.

68. Whenever a company is formed in column of platoons, or line of platoons in column of squads, the fourth and fifth sergeants place themselves as guides of their platoons as soon as practicable; they return to their posts in the line of file-closers when the company unites in line or columns of squads, unless they mark an alignment.

69. In column of subdivisions the guide of the leading subdivision is charged with the step and direction; the guides in rear preserve the trace, step, and distance.

Whenever a guide is forced out of the direction, he recovers it gradually; the guides in rear conform successively to his movements.

70. When marching in column of subdivisions, in route step and at ease, the guides maintain the trace and distance.

71. Being in column at full distance at a halt, if the guides do

not cover or have not 'their proper distances, to correct them the major establishes the guide of the leading company and the guide next in rear, in the desired direction, and commands: 1. *Right* (or *left*) *guides*, 2. *Cover.* The designated guides place themselves covering the first two, each at full distance from the guide next in front; the adjutant and sergeant-major assure them in their positions.

72.   Distance is open space measured in the direction of depth— *i. e.,* from head to rear of any formation.

73.   Interval is the open space between elements in the same line, as, the interval between files, between companies in line, between battalions in line.

74.   The following are the intervals prescribed in the Drill Regulations for organizations:

Between companies, the interval is three paces, measured from guide to guide.

Between battalions, the interval is twenty-four paces, measured from guide to guide.

Between companies in extended order, the interval is fifteen paces.

Between regiments in brigade, the interval is forty-eight paces.

Between companies in line of platoon columns, the full interval is platoon front and three paces; the close interval is eight paces.

Between squads in extended order, the normal interval is about fifteen paces.

Between sections in extended order, the normal interval is about forty-five paces; between sections of two squads each, about thirty paces.

75.   The following are the distances prescribed in the Drill Regulations:

Between platoons, the distance is platoon front.

Between companies, full distance in column of subdivisions is such that in forming line to the right or left, the subdivisions will have their proper intervals; in column of companies, it is company distance and three paces. Between companies in close column, the distance is eight paces.

76. For battalion movements, guides should perfect themselves in judging accurately the three paces, five paces, eight paces, and company distance prescribed for the various formations.

77. In successive formations into line, the guides of each company should post themselves on the line in approximately their proper positions, and should then change their positions to conform to the movements of the preceding companies until their own company arrives on the line. As the latter approaches, the guide farthest from the point of rest should glance toward the company and, if necessary, close up or open out to the proper company distance, being careful not to get out of the line of the guides.

78. After a company is halted and begins to dress, its guides should stand fast, never allowing themselves to be pushed out of position by the movements of the men in dressing.

78a. In all movements of the company in battalion, where it is prescribed that the guides leave the company and precede it by about twenty paces on the line, they should be careful to move forward together. This may be done if the guide of the company on the flank away from the point of rest watches the guide on the other flank—*i. e.*, towards the point of rest, and starts at the instant the latter starts. They then hasten—that is, they run—toward the line, halt facing to the front, take the order arms together, and face toward the point of rest. This does not, of course, apply to the movements on right into line, for the reason that the two guides have different distances to travel and must start at different times.

78b. In battalion movements, in executing on right or left into line, either from column of squads or companies, the guides of the companies in rear of the leading one must be careful to preserve the original direction of march—*i. e.*, parallel to the new line; otherwise, the execution of the movement by the company is interfered with.

CHAPTER IV.

THE NONCOMMISSIONED OFFICER IN EXTENDED ORDER.

79. The squad is the basis of extended order. Men will be taught to regard the squad as the unit from which they ought never to be separated; but if the squad should be broken up or the men become separated, they place themselves under the orders of the nearest leader and remain with his squad as if it were the one to which they originally belonged.

80. Officers and noncommissioned officers give their attention to preserving the integrity of the squads; they appoint new leaders to replace those disabled, organize new squads when necessary, and see that every man is placed in a squad.

81. In instruction in extended order, the movements must be made with reference to an enemy supposed to be in an indicated direction. The enemy is said to be *imaginary* when his position and force are merely assumed; *outlined* when his position and force are indicated by a few men only; *represented* when a body of troops acting as such has his supposed force and position.

82. Men in extended order fix their attention at the first word of command, the first note of the trumpet, or the first motion of the signal; the movement commences immediately upon completion of the command, trumpet call, or signal.

83. Extended order may be taken from any formation.

84. Upon arriving on the line and upon halting, men in extended order face to the front, whether in squads or as individual skirmishers.

85. No commands for dressing are given in extended order; the general alignment is taken toward the base file; the men stand and march at ease and pay close attention.

86. When necessary for any chief to leave his post, he will return as soon as possible.

87. In the extended order drill of the company, the sergeants are the chiefs of sections and the corporals are the squad leaders.

88. In the normal company, the second sergeant is chief of the first section; the fourth sergeant is chief of the second section; the fifth sergeant is chief of the third section; the third sergeant is chief of the fourth section. The corporals are the leaders of the squads to which they belong or with which they are marching.

89. In the exercises in leading the squad, the movements are executed at the signals of the corporal, and as far as possible without commands or cautions.

90. The movements are executed in the most direct manner, first in quick time, then in double time, finally at a run; they should not succeed each other so rapidly as to produce confusion.

91. The squad is exercised in turning, marching to the front, rear, and by the flank, obliquing, halting, deploying, and assembling, etc. In these exercises, the signals prescribed in the Drill Regulations will be used and will be thoroughly explained and illustrated to the squads by the squad leaders.

92. The man in front of whom the corporal places himself is the guide of the squad, and follows in the trace of the corporal at a distance of three paces. When the corporal does not want the squad to follow him, he commands: 1. *Guide, center*, and indicates the point of direction; if marching by the flank, he indicates the direction.

93. Before giving commands for increasing or diminishing intervals, or assembling, the corporal indicates the file who is to be the base. This indication may be made by placing himself three paces in front of such file, or by oral designation.

On halting, the corporal places himself three paces in rear of his squad, if it is acting alone. When the squad is in line of squads the corporal is three paces in front, whether marching or at a halt; and if deployed as skirmishers, he is the left skirmisher.

94. The post of a sergeant is opposite the center of his section; three paces in rear of the rear rank when the squads are assembled, and the line of skirmishers when the squads are deployed. Sergeants not in command of sections are on the same line, in the same relative position as in close order.

95. The post of a corporal when the squads are assembled is three paces in front of the base file of his squad; when the squads are deployed he takes his place as left skirmisher of his squad. If his squad is detached, he follows the principles of the School of the Squad.

96. The squad is deployed forward when it is in rear of the line to be occupied, and by the flank when it is already on that line. If the squad be at a halt, it is placed in march before deploying forward. If the squad be in march, it is halted before being deployed by the flank.

97. The normal interval between skirmishers is two paces; when a greater or less interval is used, it will be stated in the preparatory command.

98. The deployment as skirmishers is made on the front-rank men of the second file from the right (No. 2). The rear men place themselves on the alignment to the right of their file leaders, each, as soon as there is interval.

99. If the squad is to kneel or lie down upon halting, the corporal gives the cautionary command, *Kneel* (or *Lie down*), upon halting, before giving commands for deploying. The squad will then kneel (or lie down) at each halt until otherwise directed.

100. Officers and noncommissioned officers exact from the men obedience of the following rules:

a. Never fire unless ordered.

b. Never exceed the number of cartridges indicated.

c. Never fire after the command or signal *Cease firing.*

d. Always fire at the named objective; if so situated as to be unable to see the objective, do not fire.

e. Always aim at the bottom line of the objective; if it be a line of men, aim at the feet; if a clump of trees, aim at the junction of tree trunks and ground.

Scouts, from the nature of their duties, are given greater latitude. They are permitted to carry their pieces loaded and at the ready, and the question of firing is left largely to their judgment. It is frequently necessary for them to fire in self-defense, to give the alarm or to avail themselves of opportunity to fire upon leaders of the enemy.

101. The instructor will give the closest attention to the execution of the firings, and always exact the most rigid fire discipline.

102. The firings are always executed at a halt. In advancing to the attack, skirmishers lie down on being halted. Those who cannot see the objective rise to the kneeling or sitting position; and of these, those who cannot see the objective rise to the standing position.

103. For the firings, the post of the instructor is three paces in rear of the squad, but in actual firing he places himself where he can best make himself heard and at the same time best observe the effects of the fire.

104. The instructor should exercise the greatest of care in the proper giving of all commands for firings. He should thoroughly familiarize himself with the commands as prescribed in Drill Regulations, never varying therefrom. He should bear in mind that every command for firing should consist of the following parts in the following order:

1. That portion of the command that indicates the kind of fire; as: 1. *Squad,* 2. *Load.* (*Indicating Volley Firing*) 1. *Fire at will, Fire* (*so many*) *rounds,* etc.

2. That portion that indicates the range at which the men are to fix their sights; as, *At* (*so many*) *yards.*

3. That portion of the command that indicates the object at which the squad is to direct its fire; as, *At line of men,* or, *At line of woods,* etc.

4. That portion which is necessary for the loading, aiming, and firing; viz.: 1. *Ready,* 2. *Aim,* 3. *Squad,* 4. *Fire,* 5. *Load.*

105. For volley firing, the squad being in line facing the object to be fired upon, the pieces loaded and in any position: 1. *At (so many) yards,* 2. *At (such object),* 3. *Ready,* 4. *Aim,* 5. *Squad,* 6. *Fire.*

To fire another volley at the same objective with the same range: 1. *Load,* 2. *Aim,* 3. *Squad,* 4. *Fire.*

To fire another volley at the same objective, but with a new range: 1. *At (so many) yards,* 2. *Aim,* 3. *Squad,* 4. *Fire.* 5, *Load.*

To fire another volley at a new objective with a new range: 1. *At (so many) yards,* 2. *At (such and such an object),* 3. *Ready,* 4. *Aim,* 5. *Squad,* 6. *Fire,* 7. *Load.*

106. The objective and range will be indicated in the preparatory commands for all kinds of fire, as illustrated in the preceding examples.

If the objective be at a considerable angle to the front of the squad, the instructor will change the front of the squad so as to face it.

The commands are given at sufficient intervals to allow them to be executed as already prescribed. The command *Fire* is given when the pieces appear to be steady.

107. More than three volleys will rarely be fired without intermission; this is to allow the smoke to clear away, to steady the men, and to prevent the waste of ammunition.

108. To fire at will: 1. *Fire at will,* 2. *At (so many) yards,* 3. *At (such object),* 4. *Commence firing.*

At the fourth command those skirmishers who can see the enemy aim deliberately, fire, load, and continue the firing until the command or signal *Cease firing.*

The corporal may permit a few men only, usually the best shots, to fire; for this purpose he calls the men by name and then gives the same commands as before; the intensity of the fire is thus regulated by varying the number of the men firing.

109. To fire as skirmishers with counted cartridges: 1. *Fire one (two, or three) rounds,* 2. *At (so many) yards,* 3. *At (such an object),* 4. *Commence firing.*

At the fourth command those skirmishers who can see the enemy commence firing. Each man, after firing the number of cartridges, executes cease firing.

To fire another series, *Fire one (two, or three) rounds.*

The instructor will see that the number of cartridges indicated is never exceeded.

110. In the rapid fire, the number of cartridges is not limited; when used in advancing to the attack, the instructor orders bayonets fixed and sights laid down, and then commands: 1. *Rapid fire,* 2. *Commence firing.*

111. Halts are habitually made with a view: 1st, to effective fire upon the objective; 2d, to distances necessary to pass over; 3d, to the time and gaits required; 4th, to cover. *All other considerations give way to those of effective fire.*

112. In a line of sections, squads, or skirmishers, the chief of section is six paces in rear of the center of his section. When the section acts as the support in the battle formation of a company, the post of the chief of section is six paces in front of the center of his section.

113. In forming a line of squads or skirmishers, the chiefs of sections place themselves in rear of their base squads in line, or abreast of them in column; they see that the base squads keep the line of direction. The corporals take their posts in front of their squads, in line at the preparatory command for forming line of squads; in deploying as skirmishers, they take or keep their places in ranks, retaining supervision of their squads.

CHAPTER V.

ADVANCE AND REAR GUARD DUTY.*

114. An advance guard is a body of troops thrown out in front of a marching column to cover its movements, to prevent surprise, and to gain information.

115. Rear guards are corresponding bodies in the rear of the column. In forward movements they protect the rear of the column from raiding parties or detachments, arrest stragglers, prevent pillaging, etc.

116. In retreat they cover the column, checking the enemy, and delaying him so as to insure the safety of the column.

117. Troops marching in a hostile territory are preceded on the march by an advance guard and are followed by a rear guard.

A column of troops on the march consists, therefore, of an advance guard, the main body, a rear guard, and, if necessary, flanking parties.

118. In general terms, the objects of the advance guard are to observe and to resist; specifically, they are:

1. To provide for the security of the main body by giving it time to deploy when the enemy is encountered.

2. To clear the way for the main body and prevent its march being delayed.

3. To seize and hold important points until the arrival of the main body.

4. To support the cavalry screen, if there be one in front of the column.

119. The strength of the advance guard varies with the strength

---

*The material for this chapter taken from "The Service of Security and Information," by the late Colonel Arthur L. Wagner, Assistant Adjutant-General, U. S. Army, by permission of the author.

Company of Infantry as Advance Guard.

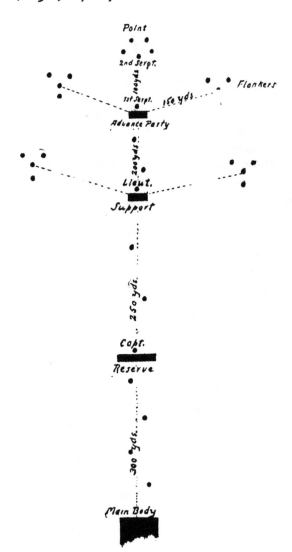

Company of Infantry as Advance Guard.

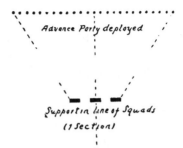

Advance Party deployed

Support in line of Squads
(1 Section)

1 Platoon   Reserve in Column
of Fours

Main Body

of the main body, the object of the march, and the nature of the country through which the column is passing. As a general rule, the strength of the advance guard may be placed at one-sixth of the whole force. This may be reduced to one-eighth for small commands.

120. An advance guard consists of a series of detachments increasing progressively in size from front to rear, each being charged with the duty of protecting from surprise the body immediately following it and gaining time for the latter to prepare for action.

121. The advance guard is divided into two parts: the reserve and the vanguard. The reserve consists of from one-third to one-half the entire advance guard. The remainder constitutes the vanguard, which is divided into the advance party and the support, the support being generally twice the size of the advance party.

122. When a single company forms the advance guard, the first section constitutes the advance party, the second section the support, and the second platoon the reserve.

123. The company being in column of squads at a halt, the captain commands: 1. *Form advance guard,* 2. *March.*

At the first command the first sergeant takes command of the first section, and the corporal of the first squad exchanges places with his rear-rank man.

At the command *March,* the front rank of the first squad, under command of the second sergeant, moves to the front as the point.

The rear rank of the first squad obliques to the left to form a flanking group.

The front rank of the second squad obliques to the right to form a flanking group.

124. The point and flankers all move out at the double time, reducing the pace to quick time when they have gained their proper distances.

125. The first sergeant detaches two men of the rear rank of the second squad to march as connecting files between the advance

party and the support, puts the other two in the file-closers, and commands: 1. *Forward,* 2. *March,* the second command being given as soon as the point has gained its proper distance.

126. The first lieutenant (remaining with the second section) commands: 1. *Forward,* 2. *March.* The second command being given as soon as the advance party has its proper distance. He then adds: 1. *Rear squad,* 2. *Right and left oblique,* 3. *March.* The front rank of the rear squad obliques to the right, the rear rank to the left, at double time, forming the flankers of the support, and taking quick time on gaining their positions.

127. The captain (remaining with the second platoon) gives the command: 1. *Forward,* 2. *March,* the second command being given as soon as the support has advanced its proper distance. If necessary, flankers may be thrown out from the reserve by the same commands and means as from the support.

128. The entire advance guard marches habitually at attention.

129. If the command is: 1. *Form advance guard,* 2. *Double time,* 3. *March,* the point and flankers move out as already prescribed, but do not reduce their pace upon gaining their positions. The advance party, the support, and the reserve move forward successively at the double time. The reserve takes the quick time at the command of the captain and the other parts of the advance guard conform to the movements of the reserve.

130. To assemble the advance guard, the reserve is halted and the other parts of the advance guard at once halt. The command: 1. *Assemble,* 2. *March,* is then given, or the signal for assembly is given. This command is repeated by the commanders of the advance party and the vanguard, and at the command *March,* all parts of the advance guard move toward the reserve by the shortest line and take their places in column.

131. Upon the receipt of an order to form a company as a rear guard, its captain halts it, and, if it be not already in that formation, forms it in column of squads facing the enemy or to the rear. The

Formation for a
Flanking Group.

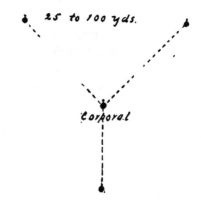

main body having gained the proper distance, the captain commands: 1. *Form rear guard*, 2. *Second platoon, squads right about*,
3. *March*, and the second platoon, under command of the captain,
at once moves to the rear and follows the main body. At the
command: 1. *First and rear squads*, 2. *Right and left oblique*,
3. *March*, the designated squads move out as flankers in the manner prescribed for the advance guard, the front rank to the right
and the rear rank to the left.

132. When the reserve has gained its proper distance, the
first lieutenant commands: 1. *Second section*, 2. *Squads left about*,
3. *March*, and it follows the reserve as a support, maintaining the
proper distance. Flankers are sent out from the rear squads as in
the advance guard.

133. The support having gained its proper distance, the first
sergeant commands: 1. *Form rear party*, 2. *March*. At the first
command, the corporal of the first squads exchanges places with his
rear-rank man, and at the command *March*, the rear rank of the
first squad and the front rank of the second squad face to the left
and right respectively, leave the column at the double time, and,
upon gaining their proper interval from the column, march to the
rear at the quick time. The front rank of the first squad stands fast.

134. Immediately after giving the command for forming the rear
party, the first sergeant commands: 1. *Squads left about*, 2. *March*,
and afterwards detaches two men as connecting files between the
rear party and the support. The front rank of the first squad,
under command of the second sergeant, assumes the proper formation for the rear point, and marches to the rear as soon as the rear
party has gained the proper distance.

135. While at a halt, each part of the advance guard remains
in its place. All parts of the advance guard should, while at a halt,
face in the supposed direction of the enemy.

136. The point and advance party are charged with the duty
of observing and investigating everything suspicious in character

on or near the line of march of the column.   They should be constantly on the alert for any and all signs of the enemy, and should make immediate reports of his whereabouts, when discovered, to the commander of the vanguard.   They should, without unnecessarily delaying the advance of the main body, investigate all houses, ravines, woods, or other places likely to afford concealment to the enemy along the line of march.

137.   The flankers are charged with a similar duty on their respective flanks, and they will exercise especial vigilance in investigating all places where the enemy might conceal themselves and deliver a flank attack on the main body.

138.   When it becomes necessary for the different parts of the advance guard to communicate with each other, they will do so by means of the prescribed or prearranged signals, and without necessary shouting or firing.

139.   Flanking parties should be under the command of non-commissioned officers or experienced privates, and in advancing they should take up the formation shown in the diagram—*i. e.,* two men in front and one in rear of the group leader.   The distances by which these men will be separated will depend on the nature of the country through which the flanking party is passing, being much greater in an open country than in a rough, broken country.

140.   The example heretofore given of the order of march of a small advance guard serves equally well for a type of a rear guard of the same strength if it be considered as faced to the rear throughout.

141.   In order to save unnecessary marching on the part of the point, advance party, and support, it may, under certain circumstances, be advantageous to assemble the advance guard on the point.   The arrival of the advance guard in camp would be such a circumstance.   The point, acting under instructions previously received or in response to pre-arranged signals, would halt at the designated point.   The other parts of the advance guard, at the command of their respective chiefs, move by the shortest lines on the point and take their proper positions in column.

CHAPTER VI.

THE NONCOMMISSIONED OFFICER IN COMMAND OF PATROLS.*

142. A patrol consists of from three to nine men under the command of a noncommissioned officer or experienced private. It is desirable that at least one member of the patrol speak the language of the country in which the army is operating.

143. The patrol commander should be given clear and definite instructions as to the duty to be performed, and he should be required to repeat them to the members of the patrol in the presence of the officer giving them.

144. These instructions should inform him: 1. The object of the reconnaissance. 2. What is known about the enemy. 3. The nature of the ground over which he is to reconnoiter. 4. The direction or directions in which he is to reconnoiter. 5. How long he is to remain out. 6. Where his reports are to be sent. 7. If other patrols are to be sent out at the same time, the particular route he is to follow.

145. The patrol commander must be certain that he understands his instructions thoroughly. If he has the slightest doubt, he should ask for a repetition of his orders.

146. He then inspects the patrol, being careful that each man has the proper amount of ammunition, and that none are sick, intoxicated, or foot-sore. Any member of the patrol having a cold that causes him to cough will be replaced. He will see that the arms and accouterments of the patrol are so arranged that they do not rattle or glisten.

147. He then points out to the patrol the positions of their own

---

*The material for this chapter taken from "The Service of Security and Information," by Colonel Arthur L. Wagner, Assistant Adjutant-General, U. S. Army, by permission of the author.

Patrols.

n.c.o.

Patrol of 3 men

n.c.o.

Patrol of 4 men

n.c.o.

Patrol of 5 men

N.C.O.

Patrol of 6 men

n.c.o.

Patrol of 7 men

n.c.o.

Patrol of 8 men

forces, and indicates a place of assembly in case the patrol should become dispersed or members lost therefrom.   He explains the signals to be used, and cautions the men that they are not to talk unnecessarily, and in whispers when they do; that they must not smoke or make a light of any kind.

148.   When on the march, the patrol should have the general formation of a main body, advance guard, rear guard, and flankers, even if the different parts are represented by one man only.   If necessary to dispense with any of these parts, the flankers should first be dispensed with.

149.   The patrol must always be so formed as to facilitate the gaining of information, and to insure, if possible, the escape of at least one man, if the patrol should be cut off.

150.   The distances between the members of the patrol depend upon circumstances.   They are rarely less than twenty-five or more than one hundred yards.   The men should be close enough to see and hear each other's signals and for mutual support.

151.   When practicable, the point should consist of two men, one to scout vigilantly toward the enemy, the other to watch for signals from the other members of the patrol.

152.   The members of the patrol should endeavor to always keep the point in view, or, in case of a large patrol, each man should endeavor to keep in sight the man next him toward the point.

153.   The patrol moves cautiously, but not timidly, along hedges, walls, ditches, ravines, etc., seeking in every way to see without being seen.   It halts frequently to listen, observe, and get the bearings of the patrol.   The commander should take notice of landmarks and directions, in order that he may not lose his way.

154.   The patrol should, if practicable, return by a different route than the one followed on advance, as it thus extends the ground over which it reconnoiters and lessens the chance of being cut off.

155.   Patrols should be careful not to move along great roads

when it is possible to observe them carefully without doing so. They will not ordinarily enter villages, but will turn them and observe them carefully.

156. The patrol should not halt to rest before its return, unless it is imperatively necessary to do so. In such case it should rest in concealment in some place which offers advantages for defense and for retreat.

157. During the day a patrol should march along high ground from which an extensive view may be obtained. At night it should be on low ground, so as to bring approaching people into view on the sky-line.

158. If one patrol meets another of the same force, the commanders should exchange information. Friendly patrols should recognize each other quietly. At night they will challenge and demand the parole and countersign.

159. When a patrol encounters a hostile patrol, it is generally better to remain in concealment than to attack. When, however, a hostile patrol has penetrated so far as to make it probable that they have gained important information, an attempt should be made to surprise and capture it.

160. If the patrol is attacked, it should return the attack boldly, and, if defeated, should disperse, each man making his way back to the rendezvous designated beforehand. If they encounter a large force, they should retreat, keeping up a lively fusillade in order to give warning.

161. If challenged by a hostile sentinel, the patrol should remain halted and silent. If challenged a second time, it should endeavor to sneak away, unless it has orders to capture prisoners, when a sudden rush should be made with a view to capturing the sentinel before assistance can reach him.

162. Upon the approach of inhabitants of the country, the patrol remains in concealment. Should they prove to be civilians coming from the direction of the enemy, they should be carefully

questioned as to the whereabouts of the enemy, what the enemy is doing, his probable strength and condition, whether he has patrols out, and any information as to the location of roads leading to the enemy.

163. People going in the direction of the enemy should be halted and never permitted to pass unless they have passes from undoubted authority.

164. If it becomes necessary to take a guide from among the people of the country, he should be treated kindly, but should be warned that any treachery will be promptly and severely punished.

165. A patrol coming to a cross-roads should investigate each road, sending two men in each direction to the first turn of the road. If anything is seen, one man returns quickly to report while the other remains to observe. The same precautions will be observed in regard to heights.

166. In case of a defile which cannot be reconnoitered, or a bridge or ford where all of the patrol cross at the same place, the patrol passes through in single file and at double time. In passing through woods, the patrol should be deployed over as large a front as possible with safety and the wood passed in this manner. Upon arriving on the farther edge of the wood, the patrol should remain concealed and observe carefully before passing out to the open ground.

167. Enclosures, such as gardens, parks, cemeteries, and houses, should be approached and examined by one or two members of the patrol, the rest of the patrol remaining in concealment where they can observe and, if necessary, assist.

168. A patrol should exercise great vigilance in entering a village. A general formation for so doing would be to enter in single file, at proper distances for observation and support, each man being on the opposite side of the street from his predecessor. If the patrol is strong enough, it should seize the postoffice, telegraph office, and railroad station, and secure all important papers that may be there.

169. The best time to enter a village is at day-break, when it is light enough to see and before the inhabitants are awake.

170. If the patrol advances to the enemy's position, it will endeavor to ascertain all information concerning the length and direction of the position, the number and positions of the sentinels, the number and positions of the pickets, the roads leading to the position from the front and from the flanks, and whether the enemy is making any changes in his dispositions.   If possible, a position on the enemy's flank will be taken up and information as to location of the troops obtained.

171. If the patrol encounters the enemy on the march, it should take up a position where it will be concealed and beyond the reach of the enemy's flankers, and observe the progress of the column, endeavoring to estimate its strength and its rate of marching.   In selecting a place of concealment, the patrol should be careful to avoid any conspicuous places, even if considerable distances from the line of march of the hostile column, as they would in all probability be searched.   The commander of the patrol should send messengers back constantly and should not hesitate to send back even his last man, if the importance of the information demand it.

172. Reports should be sent back whenever anything of importance is seen.   If in doubt as to the importance, a report should be sent.   These reports may be written or oral.   If oral, the messenger should be required to repeat the report before starting, in order to be sure that he understands it.   In case of an important message in a country where the enemy is numerous, it is best to send the same message by several men.

173. Written reports should be confined to facts, legibly written, and brief.   No more should be said than is necessary to state the facts clearly and explicitly.

CHAPTER VII.

ESCORTS.*

174. An escort is a detachment of troops detailed to accompany and afford protection to supplies, or to officials travelling in a hostile territory, or to conduct and guard prisoners.

175. The size and composition of escorts depend on various factors. A large and valuable train, a paymaster with his funds, or an important official, requires a large escort. When in the vicinity of an active enemy, a large escort is necessary. When in an open country, cavalry will be more in demand; while in a close, rugged country, infantry will preferably perform this duty.

176. Generally speaking, an escort on the march consists of a main body, an advance guard, rear guard, and flankers.

177. Escorts commanded by noncommissioned officers will generally consist of from five to twenty men and will be for the purpose of guarding a small train or a small number of prisoners. For larger and more important escorts, a commissioned officer would be detailed. Escorts of an insane patient or of one or two prisoners may consist of a noncommissioned officer and one or more privates.

178. The commander of an escort will first inspect his detail to see that the members thereof are properly armed and equipped; that none are sick, foot-sore, or intoxicated; that they are properly rationed for the trip; he will then report to the post adjutant for instructions. He then proceeds to the place where the train or the prisoners are waiting and gives instructions for the forming of the escort.

179. Upon passing the line of sentinels of the camp or garrison,

---

*In this chapter "Organization and Tactics," by Colonel Arthur L. Wagner, Assistant Adjutant-General, U. S. Army, was freely used for much of the material on the subject of escorts and convoys in hostile territory.

Escort of 7 men
for Small Train.

So. to. 100 yds.

So. to. 100 yds.

Commander of Escort

So. to. 100 yds.

Escort of 7 men when
Flankers are impracticable.

                        ▲

Commander of Escort

he causes the point and flankers to be thrown out and directs a portion of the escort to remain behind as a rear guard. The remainder of the escort under the commander of the escort takes its position in front of the train.

180. The point, flankers, and rear guard should compose about half of the escort, the other half constituting the main body.

181. The point, flankers, and rear guard should be at such a distance from the train as to prevent its being surprised, but should not be so far away as to permit of being cut off from the main body. It is best however, to be far enough in advance to discover and engage the enemy at such a distance that he cannot throw the train into confusion.

182. An attacking force will generally try to take a train in flank. Care should be taken that a feint in front does not draw the entire escort into action, thus leaving the train open to a flank attack.

183. In passing a bridge, ford, defile, or other locality favorable for a surprise, the train should be halted until the advance guard has passed and taken up a position beyond, when the train may proceed.

184. Every member of the escort should be constantly on the alert for any and all indications of the enemy. No place of possible concealment should be passed without investigation. With small escorts, constant vigilance is the only price of safety.

185. If attacked, the enemy should be engaged and held where it is encountered—*i. e.*, at some distance from the train. If the engagement results in a victory for the escort, the pursuit, if any, should be small. If the enemy is in such force as to make a retreat necessary, care should be exercised in turning the wagons around in order to prevent their upsetting. One wagon upset in the road may block and prevent the retreat of the entire train.

186. In escorting prisoners, the strength of the escort is generally fixed at one infantry soldier for every ten prisoners. In the case of a small number of prisoners, the proportionate escort would be much larger.

187.   The escort should be formed as indicated in paragraph 179, the prisoners being placed in some convenient formation, such as column of twos, fours, etc.   In this case the main body would march in rear of the column of prisoners, with single men marching at intervals on each side of the column.

188.   If the commander of the escort does not speak the language of the prisoners, he should be provided with an interpreter who does.

189.   Prisoners should be treated with kindness and consideration, but should be given to understand that any attempt to escape, or that any offer of violence to their guard, will be promptly and severely dealt with.   They should not be permitted to hold conversation or communication with any one except their guard, and then only when necessary.

190.   At night they will be placed in enclosures or buildings, if possible, but the vigilance of the guard should in no way be relaxed.

191.   If halting for rest, or if menaced by the enemy, the prisoners will be closed in a compact mass.   The defense of a convoy of prisoners will be conducted as indicated for that of a train.

192.   In time of peace and when escorting military prisoners, a noncommissioned officer will, upon the receipt of the order, report to the post adjutant for instructions.   He will then report with his order to the post quartermaster for the necessary transportation. If the journey is to be of more than one day's duration and the order does not direct otherwise, he will report to the post commissary for rations for himself and escort, or commutation thereof.

193.   He forms and inspects his detail as prescribed in paragraph 178, and proceeds to the designated place to receive the prisoners.   He carefully verifies their number and receipts for the same. Having once received them, he becomes responsible for their safe-keeping, and will make such disposition of his escort as will in his opinion insure their safe-guarding.   In case of a small escort, or

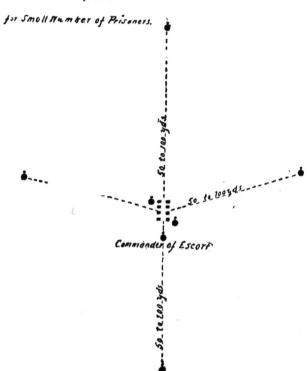

Escort of 7 men
for Small Number of Prisoners.

Escort of 7 Men

When Flankers are

impracticable

50 to 100 yds

Commander of Escort

50 to 100 yds

where it is necessary to conduct the prisoners through a crowded district favorable for escape, such as depots, ferries, etc., or where the prisoners are desperate characters, and an attempt at escape is apprehended, it would be best to handcuff the prisoners in pairs, and, if necessary, handcuff the pairs to members of the escort.

194. In receiving military prisoners, the commander of the escort will be careful to verify the list of clothing and other articles of public property in their possession. While under his charge, he is responsible that they do not discard or lose any of these articles. The list should be again verified when the prisoners are turned over at their destination.

195. When on trains or boats, a sentinel should always be posted over the prisoners, especially at night. When any one prisoner is separated from the rest—to go to the water-closet, etc.—he should always be accompanied by a sentinel, with instructions to keep the prisoner constantly in sight.

196. In conducting the prisoners and while waiting in depots, ferries, etc., it is best to select some inconspicuous position and avoid being an object of public curiosity.

197. Upon arrival at the destination, the party will proceed to the office of the post adjutant, or, if it be a prison, to the office of the officer in charge, and the commander of the escort will report his arrival. In reporting, the commander of the escort should say: "Sir, Sergeant (or Corporal) So-and-So, Co. ——, —— Infantry, reports his arrival from Fort —— with (so many) prisoners." He will then dispose of his prisoners as directed by the official, taking a receipt for them. Having turned over his prisoners, he will then report to the proper authorities for subsistence and transportation for himself and escort to their proper station.

198. Upon return to his proper station, he will report his return to the post adjutant and turn in the receipt for the prisoners.

199. While *en route*, the commander of the escort will not permit the use of intoxicants by either the members of the escort or

by the prisoners, and he will not permit them to annoy or disturb the public by noisy or disorderly conduct.

200. If it should become necessary to remain over night in cities, towns, or other localities where it is impossible to properly guard the prisoners under his charge, the commander of the escort will make application at a police station or jail for permission to lock his prisoners up for the night.

201. An insane soldier will be escorted by a noncommissioned officer. When a number are sent at one time, or when the patient or patients are violent, the department commander may order such addition to the escort as may be necessary. The noncommissioned officer will report to the Adjutant-General of the Army by telegraph, at least twenty-four hours in advance, the probable time and place of his arrival in Washington. After leaving his patient at the asylum, the noncommissioned officer will report to the Adjutant-General of the Army for instructions. A. R. 467.

202. Upon receipt of the order for this duty, the noncommissioned officer will report, as prescribed in paragraph 192, for instructions, subsistence, and transportation.

203. If, upon arrival in Washington, there is neither transportation nor instructions awaiting the noncommissioned officer at the place of arrival, he should remain at that point and telephone the Adjutant-General's office for instructions.

204. While traveling or waiting in public places, the noncommissioned officer should endeavor to make himself and his patient or patients as inconspicuous as possible.

205. The funeral escort of a noncommissioned staff officer will consist of sixteen men, commanded by a sergeant; of a sergeant, fourteen men, commanded by a sergeant; of a corporal, twelve men, commanded by a corporal; of a private, eight men, commanded by a corporal. A. R. 428.

206. A funeral escort is formed opposite the tent or quarters of the deceased, the band being on the flank of the escort toward which

it is to march.   Upon the appearance of the coffin, the commander of the escort commands: 1. *Present,*   2. *Arms,* and the band plays an appropriate air.   Arms are then brought to the order, after which the coffin is taken to the flank of the escort opposite the music.

207.   If the escort be small, as in the case of the escort of an enlisted man, the escort may be marched in line.   The procession being formed, the commander of the escort puts it in march, arms at the right shoulder.

208.   The escort marches slowly to solemn music; the column having arrived opposite the grave, line is formed facing it.   The coffin is then carried along the front of the escort to the grave, arms are presented, the music plays an appropriate air; the coffin having been placed over the grave, the music ceases and the arms are brought to the order.

209.   The commander of the escort next commands: 1. *Parade,* 2. *Rest.*   The escort executes parade rest, the officers and men inclining the head to the front.

210.   When the funeral services are completed and the coffin lowered into the grave, the commander of the escort causes the escort to resume attention and fire three rounds of blank cartridges, the muzzles of the pieces being elevated.

211.   The escort will be brought to attention by the command: 1. *Escort,*   2. *Attention.*   To fire the volleys, the commands are as follows: 1. *With blank cartridges,*   2. *Squad,*   3. *Load,*   4. *Ready,* 5. *Aim,*   6. *Squad,*   7. *Fire,*   8. *Load.*   When three volleys have been fired, the command: 1. *Cease,*   2. *Firing,* will be given.   After the trumpeter has sounded "Taps," the escort is formed into column, marched in quick time to the point where it was assembled, and dismissed.

212.   When the distance to the place of interment is considerable, the escort, after having left the camp or garrison, may march at ease until it approaches the burial-ground, when it is called to attention.

213.   When necessary to escort the remains from the quarters

of the deceased to the church before the funeral service, arms are presented upon receiving the remains at the quarters, and also as they are borne into the church.

214.   When escorting the remains to some point for transportation, the escort presents arms while the remains are being transferred from the hearse and embarked for transportation.

CHAPTER VIII.

Outpost Duty.*

215. Outposts are detachments thrown out from a force, when halted, to protect it from surprise. Like advance guards on the march, outposts are charged with the duty of observation and resistance. They prevent reconnaissance of the position by the enemy's scouts and patrols, give warning of the approach of the enemy, and offer sufficient resistance to the enemy's attacks to enable the main body to prepare for action.

216.   The duties of the outposts may be classified as follows:

1.   Observation: To observe constantly all approaches by which the enemy might advance; to watch and immediately report the movements of the enemy.

2.   Resistance: To prevent reconnaissance by the enemy; above all, to check the advance of the enemy long enough to enable the main body to prepare for action.

217.   The outpost is divided into four parts—namely: (1) Sentinels or vedettes, (2) pickets, (3) supports, (4) reserve. The sentinels occupy the line of observation; the supports usually occupy the line of resistance.

218.   The strength of the reserve varies from one-third to one-half of the entire outpost, the rest of the outpost constituting the supports and pickets. Each picket depends on the number of sentinels and patrols it has to furnish, and each support should be equal to the aggregate of all the pickets it supports.

219.   The outpost should cover the front of the force it is protecting and overlap its flanks unless they are protected by impassable obstacles.

---

*The material for this chapter is taken from "The Service of Security and Information," by the late Colonel Arthur L. Wagner, Assistant Adjutant-General, U. S. Army, by permission of the author.

Outpost

Line of Pickets omitted

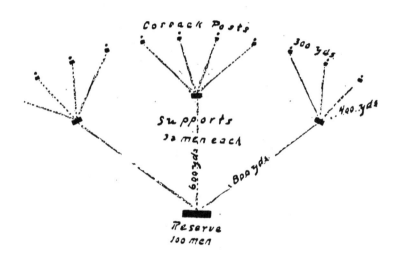

Cossack Posts

300 yds

Supports
32 men each

400.yds

600 yds

800 yds

Reserve
100 men

Outpost Composed of Battalion of Infantry

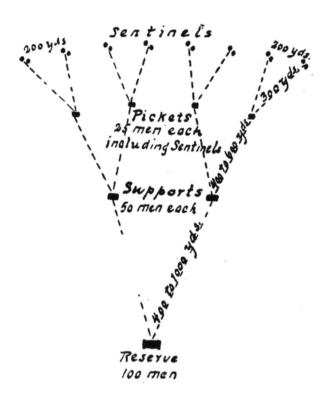

Sentinels

200 yds. 200 yds. 300 yds.

Pickets
25 men each
including Sentinels

400 to 600 yds.

Supports
50 men each

400 to 1000 yds.

Reserve
100 men

220. The disposition of the parts of an outpost and the distances between the parts thereof, are shown in the accompanying plates, both of which show permissible formations for outposts.

221. The duties of noncommissioned officers on outpost will in general be confined to the command of examining posts, detached posts, Cossack posts, the posting, inspecting, instructing, and relieving of sentinels, and in the group system of posting sentinels, in the command of one or more groups.

222. An examining post is a point designated on the line of the outposts at which all persons desiring to pass the line of outposts must present themselves for examination and authority.

223. It will consist of an officer or noncommissioned officer and six men—three reliefs for one double sentinel post.

224. Upon the approach of any person to the examining post, one of the sentinels advances and halts him at some distance from the line, while the other notifies the commander of the post, who examines the stranger and either allows him to pass or conducts him to the commander of the picket.

225. Any person approaching the line of sentinels at any other than the designated point is passed along from post to post, until he is brought to the examining post. Care should be taken that such person is not afforded an opportunity to observe the location of the pickets or supports.

226. The bearers of a flag of truce will not, as a rule, be permitted to pass the line of sentinels. When such persons or other suspected persons are passed beyond the line of sentinels, they will be blindfolded.

227. The commander of an examining post should exercise the greatest care in the examination of persons before allowing them to pass, and in case of any doubt should report to the next higher authority, first blindfolding the person before sending him farther within the lines.

228. A detached post is a detail of from three to twelve men

under an officer or noncommissioned officer, detached from a picket to protect an exposed point or support an isolated sentinel.

229. A noncommissioned officer in command of a detached post should, upon arrival at the designated place, post a sentinel or sentinels so that they may best observe the surrounding country without unnecessarily exposing themselves to view. He should then place the remainder of the detachment where it will be concealed from view and at the same time be within easy reach of the sentinel.

230. He will require the men to remain under arms at all times, and will not permit noise among them. He will not permit fires to be lighted.

231. If the post be important, and it is thought that an attempt might be made by the enemy to capture it, it may be entrenched with hasty entrenchments, the fresh earth being covered by sod and the branches of trees.

232. The times and methods of posting and relieving sentinels will be prescribed by the commander of the outpost.

233. Sentinels may be posted singly or in pairs; in the latter case, both should be constantly on the alert, and when anything suspicious is observed, one should go and investigate, while the other remains on post. They should be posted far enough apart to prevent easy conversation.

234. The noncommissioned officers will see that the sentinels do not smoke, or have about them any glittering accouterments. Except in foggy weather or on a dark night, they will see that they keep their bayonets in the scabbards.

235. In instructing sentinels, they will see that each sentinel thoroughly understands the following:

1. The countersign. 2. The number of his own post. 3. The number and position of his own picket and the name of its commander. 4. The position of the neighboring sentinels and the examining post when there is one. 5. The direction of the enemy and the probable line of his advance. 6. The point to which all roads,

paths, and railroads in sight lead. 7. The names of all villages and rivers in view. 8. The signals by which he should communicate with the pickets and detached posts. 9. The principal thing is to see that the sentinel knows where to look for the enemy and what to do if he sees him.

236. Deserters from the enemy are halted at some distance from the post, and required to lay down their arms. The commander of the picket is at once notified. If the deserters are pursued by the enemy, they are ordered to halt, and if they do not do so, they are fired upon.

237. In posting sentinels, the most intelligent men should be assigned to the most important posts. It is advisable to keep men on the same posts instead of changing them to new posts each time they are posted.

238. A sentinel on post pays no compliments and takes no notice of any of his officers who come upon his post, unless addressed by them, except so far as may be necessary to challenge and identify them.

239. Outposts should, as a rule, avoid unnecessary movements tending to bring on an engagement; but, if attacked, should resist stubbornly, in order to give the main body time to prepare for action. The chief resistance is usually made on the line of the supports. The pickets will, as a general rule, advance in line of skirmishers to the line of the sentinels; the whole line then falls back to the line of the supports.

240. A Cossack post consists of four men—*i. e.*, three men and a noncommissioned officer or experienced private. When Cossack posts are used, the line of pickets is dispensed with and the posts are sent out directly from the supports.

241. When using the Cossack posts, the sentinels are posted singly, one being sent out from each post, the other two and the noncommissioned officer remaining concealed in rear and within easy distance. The sentinel is posted from ten to twenty yards in

front of the post, in a position where he can best observe the surrounding country.

242.   The members of the post should keep the sentinel in constant view.   Each fost should be intrenched and should be so stationed that it is able to cross its fire with that of the posts on both sides of it.

243.   The duties of the noncommissioned officer in command of a Cossack post are the same as those prescribed for a noncommissioned officer in command of a relief when pickets are used.

CHAPTER IX.

THE FIRST SERGEANT.

244. The first sergeant of a company or organization is selected by the company commander for his excellence of character, capacity to command the respect and obedience of the enlisted men, intelligence, efficiency, and military bearing. He assists the company commander and the commissioned officers of the company in the discipline, instruction, and administration of the company.

245. The first sergeant is the senior noncommissioned officer of the organization to which he belongs, and, in the absence of the commissioned officers, he is responsible for the preservation of order, the maintenance of discipline, and the enforcing of orders and regulations in the company.

246. He is responsible under the company commmander for the proper care and preservation of all company books and records. He will supervise the company clerk in all of the clerical work pertaining to the company, such as the preparation of rolls, reports, requisitions, and letters, and he will see that the proper and appropriate entries of all papers pertaining to or passing through the company office are made in the company books of record; he will see that the files of orders, circulars, letters, retained copies of rolls, returns, reports, etc., are properly kept.

247. He will have personal charge of all rosters of the noncommissioned officers and men of the company. He will keep these rosters and will personally make all details for duty to which the noncommissioned officers and men of the company may be subject from time to time.

248. A roster is a list of officers or men for duty, with a record of the duty performed by each. Generally, details for duty are so made that the one longest off is the first for duty. A. R. 355.

249. All details for service in garrison and in field, except the authorized special and extra-duty details, will be by roster; but officers or enlisted men, when detailed, must serve, whether a roster be kept or not. A. R. 356.

250. Rosters are distinct for each class. Sergeants, corporals, musicians, and privates form distinct rosters. Details are made in succession according to roster, beginning at the head.

251. In making details by roster, an officer or enlisted man is each day charged with the number of days that he has remained present and available for duty since his last tour. A. R. 360.

252. The first sergeant will attend all formations of the company, unless otherwise directed by the company commander or other competent authority.

253. At the sounding of the assembly, the first sergeant takes his position six paces in front of where the center of the company is to be, and, facing it, draws saber and commands: *Fall in.*

The second sergeant places himself, facing to the front, where the right of the company is to rest, and at such a point that the center of the company will be six paces from and opposite the first sergeant; the squads form, facing to the front, in their proper places on the left of the second sergeant, superintended by the other sergeants, who then take their posts.

The first sergeant commands: *Report.* Remaining in position at the order, the squad leaders, in succession from the right, salute and report: *"All present"*; or, *"Private(s) ——— absent."* The first sergeant does not return the salutes of the squad leaders.

Squads of less than six men are increased or broken up as provided for the left squad.

The first sergeant then brings his piece to the right shoulder, commands: 1. *Port,* 2. *Arms,* 3. *Open,* 4. *Chamber,* 5. *Close,* 6. *Chamber,* 7. *Order,* 8. *Arms,* faces about, salutes the captain, reports: *"Sir, all present or accounted for"*; or, the names of the unauthorized absentees, and without command takes his post, passing around the right flank.

This formation is used in the field and, as far as practicable, in camp and garrison.

When the company becomes reduced in numbers and the squads broken up, the men fall in without regard to squads but in their relative order, closing to the right so as to leave no blank files; the corporals place themselves as number four, front rank; the sergeants superintend the formation and take their posts. The first sergeant then brings the company to the right shoulder, retains the order himself, and calls the roll; each man, as his name is called, answers *"Here"* and comes to the order. The first sergeant brings his piece to the right shoulder, causes the company to count off, forms the left squad, and if the company is large enough, divides it into platoons and sections; he then brings the company to port arms, and the formation continues as explained in the preceding paragraph.

254. The post of the first sergeant, when the company is in line, is in the line of file-closers in rear of the second file from the right of the first platoon.

255. At retreat roll call, when there is no commissioned officer present with the company, the first sergeant will, after having called the roll, dress the compaany to the right, bring the company to parade rest, and, taking his position on the right of the right guide, execute parade rest. At the conclusion of retreat he will bring the company to attention and remain in this position until the completion of the playing of "The Star-Spangled Banner," when he will dismiss the company and report to the proper officer at the designated place the result of the roll call. Where one officer superintends the roll call of several companies at reveille, the company will be dismissed before the report is rendered. At formation for muster, no report of the roll call is rendered to the officer superintending the formation.

256. He will immediately after breakfast each day make up the sick report book of the company, placing therein the names of any officers, noncommissioned officers, and men of the company

who may desire medical treatment. He will report with the sick report book to the company commander in ample time to permit of its being signed and presented by the sick marcher at the hospital at sick call.

257. Upon return of the sick report from the hospital, he will make up the company morning report and will present it to the company commander for signature, together with any other papers or letters requiring his signature, before eight o'clock. When the morning report book has been signed by the company commander, the first sergeant will deliver it to the post sergeant-major at such time and place as may be designated by the post commander.

258. At first sergeant's call he will proceed to the adjutant's office and obtain the company morning report book. While there, he will inspect the bulletin-board in the office of the sergeant-major and will carefully note the particulars of all details and instructions concerning his company which may be posted thereon. He will also report to the sergeant-major for any additional instructions which the latter may have.

259. Upon returning from the adjutant's office, he will make out from the roster the company guard detail for the following day and will post a copy of the same on the company bulletin-board. This detail, together with the other details for noncommissioned officers in charge of quarters, room orderly or orderlies, and details for company fatigue or police, will be published by the first sergeant at the conclusion of the formation for retreat roll call.

260. At the assembly for guard mounting, the men warned for duty fall in on their company parade-grounds, facing to the front, noncommissioned officers and supernumeraries falling in as file-closers; each first sergeant then verifies his detail, opens ranks, inspects the dress and general appearance, replaces by a supernumcrary any man unfit to march on guard, and then closes ranks. (The detail is then marched to the vicinity of the parade-ground or other place designated for the mounting of the guard.) When ad-

jutant's call has sounded and the sergeant-major has taken his post, the band plays in quick time and the details are marched at the right shoulder by the first sergeants and halted successively on the line established by the sergeant-major; the detail that arrives first is so marched to the line that, upon halting, the breast of the right front-rank man shall be near to and opposite the left arm of the sergeant-major; the first sergeant, remaining at the right shoulder, halts his detail, places himself in front of and facing the sergeant-major at a distance equal to or a little greater than the front of his detail; he then commands: 1. *Right,* 2. *Dress.* The detail dresses up to the line of the sergeant-major and the first sergeant, the right front-rank man placing his breast against the left arm of the sergeant-major; the non-commissioned officers take post two paces and the supernumeraries nine paces in rear of the rear rank of the detail. Seeing the detail aligned, the first sergeant commands: *Front;* salutes with the rifle salute, and then reports: *"The detail is correct";* or, *"(So many) sergeants, corporals, or privates absent";* he then passes by the right of the guard and takes post three paces in rear of his supernumerary, at the order.

The details alternate in taking the right of the line.

261. The first sergeants and supernumeraries come to parade rest and attention with the guard; they remain at the order arms while the guard is being presented and formed into column. The senior first sergeant commands: 1. *Parade,* 2. *Rest,* at the command *March* for passing in review, and 1. *Supernumeraries,* 2. *Attention,* when the officers of the day come to attention. The first sergeants come to parade rest and attention with the supernumeraries. The rear of the column having passed the officers of the day, each first sergeant marches his supernumerary to the company parade and dismisses him.

262. Guard mounting, when there is but the one detail, is held as previously described; the detail is marched on as described for the first detail, the supernumeraries are distributed uniformly on

the line nine paces in rear of the rear rank, and the first sergeant places himself three paces in rear of the center of the line of supernumeraries.

263. The duties herein described for the first sergeant may be performed by other sergeants not detailed for guard.

264. After parade, the major may direct the company officers to form line in order of rank on the left of the staff, in which case the music ceases when the officers join the staff. After closing ranks, the major causes the companies to pass in review, under command of their first sergeants, by the same commands as before. The company officers return saber with the major.

265. The stopping of the music is the signal to the first sergeants that the officers are not to return and, in consequence, that they are in command of their respective companies. They should take their posts on the right of the right guides immediately, moving there and to the head of the company when column of squads is formed, at the trail and coming to the right shoulder when the men in ranks do. Each first sergeant gives the commands: 1. *Squads right,* 2. *Company,* 6. *Forward.*

A noncommissioned officer in command of a company at parade takes post, after dressing the company, on the right of the right guide.   Before bringing the company to parade rest, he comes to the trail, steps two paces to the front and faces to the left, retaining the piece at the trail; having given his commands, he resumes his post and comes to the parade rest.

In reporting, with his piece at the order, he salutes with the rifle salute and reports: "*Sir, (Such) company, present or accounted for*"; or, "*(So many) enlisted men absent.*"   After reporting, he resumes the order arms.

266. The first sergeant will at all times perform the duties of file-closer in rectifying mistakes and insuring steadiness in ranks.

267. In movements of the company from line into column and the reverse, he retains his position in rear of or on the flank of the

right four. The first sergeant always remains with the original first platoon, when in line, in rear of the second file from the outer flank, taking the corresponding position when the platoons unite in column of squads.

268. In extended order, the post of the first sergeant is in the line of sergeants, in rear of the base squad. Should the captain be called from his post in front of the base squad during the advance, the first sergeant takes such post in order that all may be constantly aware of the position of the base squad. On return of the captain, the first sergeant drops back to his post in rear of the base squad.

269. In the advance guard formation, where the company forms the advance guard of a larger body, the first sergeant is in command of the advance party. In the rear guard he commands the corresponding element of the rear guard.

270. Upon assignment to the company of a recruit or of a man transferred thereto from another organization, the first sergeant will at once enter in the books of the company the facts contained in the descriptive and assignment card or in the descriptive list of the man. He will assign him to quarters and to a squad in the company. He will have issued to him by the quartermaster-sergeant a complete equipment of ordnance and quartermaster property. He will prepare a requisition for such clothing as the recruit may need.

271. Upon the discharge of a man from the company, he will prepare the discharge and final statements of the man for the signature of the company commander or will supervise the company clerk in so doing. He will cause the man to turn in to the quartermaster-sergeant all ordnance or quartermaster property in his possession; should any be missing, he will cause the value of the missing articles to be charged against the account of the man on his final statements. When a man has been discharged, his accounts will be closed in the company books, and they will be prepared for the signature of the company commander. Should the man re-enlist, he is regarded as a recruit and new accounts opened.

272. Upon the transfer of a man from his company or the departure of a man from the post of his company for detached service, the first sergeant will at once prepare a descriptive list, setting forth the facts of his payment, the condition of his clothing allowances, and all facts necessary to the settlement of his accounts with the Government if he should be discharged. This descriptive list is forwarded to the commanding officer of the post or detachment to which the man is sent.

273. In case of the death or desertion of an enlisted man of the company, the first sergeant will at once secure the effects and Government property for which the deceased or the deserter was responsible and hold them for the action of the company commander.

274. He will, each day, make out a list of the men in the company desiring passes; he will then make out for each man a pass for the desired time and will present these passes with the morning report to the company commander for approval and signature. When signed by the company commander, they should be delivered at the adjutant's office with the morning report.

274a. The first sergeant, upon being directed by the captain to *dismiss the company*, remaining in place, brings his piece to the right shoulder and salutes, then steps three paces to the front and two paces to the right of the company and commands: 1. *Port*, 2. *Arms*, 3. *Open*, 4. *Chamber*, 5. *Close*, 6. *Chamber*, 7. *Dismissed*.

274b. The first sergeant should keep a list of the sizes of the clothing of all men in the company.

He should see that all outer clothing is properly marked with the initials of the owner and the letter of the company. This assists in preventing the sale of clothing by men of the company to recruits and others.

He should require squad leaders to keep a proper check on the clothing of the men, especially the recruits, of their squads.

He should remind the company commander to read the Articles

of War to the company, at least twice a year, generally in January and June, and to recruits within a day or two after they join.

He should keep a book, with one page to each officer and man of the company, and note therein anything such as detail to extra, special or detached duty, relief therefrom, absence with or without leave, court-martial fines, furloughs, etc.—in fact, all data which is necessary in the preparation of muster- and pay-rolls.

He should see that clothing and equipments belonging to the men of the company are arranged in an orderly and uniform manner.

After retreat each night, he should furnish the noncommissioned officer in charge of quarters with a list of the men who will be absent by authority from 11:00 p. m. inspection of quarters.

In making details for duty from the company, he should be careful that extra work is distributed equally among the members of the company, thus avoiding discontent in the company.

He should also keep the data from which the history of the company may be compiled.

SUPPLEMENTARY TO CHAPTER "THE FIRST SERGEANT."

LIST OF REPORTS AND RETURNS TO BE RENDERED BY COMMANDING OFFICERS OF COMPANIES.

DAILY.

Morning Report_____ To be delivered to the post adjutant before 8:00 a. m. To be signed by the first sergeant and the company commander. A careful record of events should be entered in the morning report each day.

Sick Report_____ To be delivered by the s i c k marcher to the attending surgeon at the post hospital at sick call. To be signed by the company commander before sending it to the hospital.

TRIMONTHLY.

Ration Return_____ To be submitted to the adjutant, with the morning report, at such times as the commanding officer may direct.

Trimonthly Field Return_____ To be submitted only when in
(In triplicate.) the field. To be submitted on the 10th, 20th, and last day of the month. One copy to the adjutant, one to the Adjutant-General direct, one to be retained.

MONTHLY.

Pay-Rolls_____ To be submitted on the last day
(In triplicate.) of the month to the adjutant for the signature of the commanding officer. Two copies for the paymaster, one to be retained.

List of Absentees from Muster___ To be submitted to the mustering officer with the muster- or payrolls, the list to be alphabetical in order, showing the place of absence and the authority for the absence of each absentee.

Arms and Ammunition on Hand_ To be submitted to the adjutant on the first day of the ensuing month. Submitted only when required by special instructions.

Vacancies to Occur in the Current
Month_____ To be submitted to the adjutant on the first day of the month.

Company Return_____ To be submitted to the adju-
(In duplicate.) tant of the regiment. Independ-
ent company in the field, one copy
direct to the Adjutant-General,
one copy to be retained. Submitted on the first day of the following month; also submitted upon leaving a station.

Allotments Commenced During
ing the Month_____ To be submitted to the Paymaster-General by registered mail
on the last day of the month.

Discontinued Allotments _____ To be submitted to the Paymaster-General on the last day of
the month.

BIMONTHLY.

Muster-Rolls_____ To be submitted to the muster-
(In duplicate.) ing officer so that they may be
mailed within three (3) d a y s.
These rolls are to be prepared in
addition to the three pay - rolls.
One copy to be retained. Submitted on the last day of Febru-
ary, April, June, August, October,
and December.

Requisition for Blank Forms_____ To be submitted so as to arrive
at the office of the Adjutant-Gen-
eral of the Department not later
than June 1st and December 1st.

Ordnance Return_____ To be submitted within twenty
days after the 30th of June and
the 31st of December, each year.
One copy with all vouchers forwarded, one copy retained.

Estimate of C l o t h i n g a n d
Equipage_____ To be submitted to the adjutant
about ten days before the end of
each quarter.

Requisition for Stationery_____ To be submitted to the quarter-
(In duplicate.)   master whenever stationery is
required.

Requisition for Brooms and Scrub-
bing Brushes_____ To be submitted to the adjutant
(In duplicate.)   on first day of each quarter for the
approval of the commanding offi-
cer, then to the quartermaster.

SEMI-ANNUALLY.

Statement of Charges for Quarter-
master Supplies_____ To be forwarded to the office of
the quartermaster on the last day
of each quarter.

AT IRREGULAR INTERVALS.

Descriptive List and Account of
Pay and Clothing of a Soldier
Transferred_____ To be mailed to the commanding officer of the organization to
which the soldier has transferred
upon departure of the soldier from
the post.

Same of Soldier Detached _____ To be given to the officer or
noncommissioned officer in charge

of soldier or forwarded by mail. To be sent when the soldier leaves the post.

Same of Sick Soldier_____ To be sent to the surgeon in charge when the soldier is detached from the company.

Same of a Deserter_____ To be mailed direct to the officer making the report of the surrender or apprehension immediately upon receipt of notification of the same.

Special Descriptive List of Deserters _____ Submitted to the adjutant as
(In quintuplicate.) soon as the deserter is dropped from the rolls.

Notification of Discharge_____ Submitted to the paymaster to whom the man is to apply for payment. Should be forwarded about a week before the discharge is to take effect. This form must be filled out by the company commander.

Deceased Soldiers_____ Submitted to the Adjutant-General of the Army direct; also notification to the nearest relative. Submitted upon notification of death. Should be accompanied by inventory of effects and final statements of the deceased.

Field Return_____ Submitted to the adjutant of the post whenever joining or leaving a station.

Deposits, List of_____ To be submitted to the Paymaster-General direct immediately following deposit. If a soldier who has deposits is transferred or deserts, a report should be made direct to the Paymaster-General.

List of Allotments_____ Submitted to the Paymaster-General direct as soon as the allotments are made.

Notification of Cessation or of
Suspension of Allotment_____ Submitted direct to the department or corps commander immediately; also to the Paymaster-General at the end of the month, a report of the allotments to be discontinued during the e n s u i n g month.

Battles or Engagements_____ Submitted through military channels to the A d j u t a n t - General, U. S. A., after every battle or engagement.

Casualties (Killed and Wounded)_ One copy to be retained, one
    (In triplicate.) submitted through military channels, and one direct to the Adjutant-General, U. S. A. To be submitted after any engagement resulting in casualties.

Captured Property, Return of____ Submitted to the Adjutant-General, U. S. A., immediately. Only required of the company commander when the company is acting alone.

Clothing Requisition_____ Submitted to the a d j u t a n t whenever clothing is needed.

Report of Small-Arms Practice__ Submitted to the inspector of small-arms practice on completion of the target practice.

Discharge for Disability_____ To the Adjutant-General of the Department. Careful attention should be given to the notes on the blank.

Certificate of Breakage of China Ware_____ To the Quartermaster at the end of each quarter.

CHAPTER X.

The Company Quartermaster-Sergeant.

275. The company quartermaster-sergeant is selected by the company commander from among the sergeants of the company to which he belongs. A separate warrant as such is not given, and he may be returned to the grade of sergeant without reference to higher authority.

276. He is usually also the "mess" sergeant, and, as such, he is in immediate charge of the company kitchen, the company mess-room, the company store-rooms, and such other portions of barracks as the company commander may direct. He has charge of the company cooks, the men detailed for duty in the company mess-room, and the kitchen police, and directs them in execution of their duties.

277. He is directly responsible to the company commander for all Government or company property in possession of the company. He has charge of and is responsible for the security of the subsistence, quartermaster, and ordnance store-rooms, and for the preservation and care of the articles stored therein. He will in person make all issues therefrom to the cooks and to the men of the company. He will make no issues whatsoever without proper authority.

278. He will keep a record in the company property book of all quartermaster and ordnance property on hand in the store-rooms or issued to the men of the company.

279. He is responsible for the cleanliness and neatness of the company kitchen, kitchen furniture, mess-room, mess-room furniture, and will see that the cooks and men detailed for duty in the mess-room are neat and cleanly in the preparing and serving of the food. He will see that the meals are served promptly and at the hours designated in orders.

280. He will, with the assistance of the company cooks, make out each day the bill of fare for the succeeding day, and will submit the same to the company commander for his inspection.

281. Once during each quarter, and oftener if necessary, he will inspect all Government property in the possession of the company and will submit for the inspection of the company commander all articles which may be found unfit for further use. He will make frequent inspections of the quarters of the company, and will report to the company commander any repairs needed in the quarters, furniture, or property of the company.

282. He will keep note of the supply of fuel and oil, and will report to the company commander in order that timely requisition may be made to renew the supply.

283. On ration days he will, with a suitable detail from the company, report at the commissary and draw the rations of the company. He will, before reporting for rations, prepare a list showing the quantities of each article which he desires to draw or leave undrawn as a saving. When articles are issued to him, he will verify the amounts and will note the quality and condition of the same. He will enter in his books an account of all subsistence stores issued to him, and will report to the company commander any deficiency in the amount or quality of the stores.

284. On the days on which fresh meat is issued, he will report, with a suitable detail from the company, at the designated time and place to receive the same, making note in his books of the quality and quantity received.

285. He will, under the direction of the company commander, make purchases from the commissary or from local dealers of articles other than those of the ration which may be desired for the company mess.

286. He will keep a careful account of all such expenditures, taking receipts for the same and turning them in with his accounts to he company commander at intervals to be designated by the latter.

287.   He will supervise the company cooks in the handling of the rations, being careful to see that the amount cooked each day is in accord with the number of men to be fed.   He will see that the articles of the ration are not wasted and that they are used only for the purpose for which they are intended.

288.   He will be present at and preserve order in the mess-rooms during the serving of meals.   He will see that the men of the company are neat and orderly in their conduct while at table.

289.   He should familiarize himself thoroughly with the different components of the ration as authorized in the Army Regulations and in orders, together with the allowances of each.   He should be able to compute readily the quantities of each component of the ration for any number of men.

CHAPTER XI.

THE NONCOMMISSIONED OFFICER IN CHARGE OF QUARTERS.

290. The noncommissioned officer in charge of quarters is detailed by order of the company commander from a roster of the noncommissioned officers of the company.

291. The tour of duty is of twenty-four hours' duration, beginning at reveille of the day designated and continuing until reveille of the following day, unless otherwise prescribed. Noncommissioned officers detailed for this duty relieve each other without reporting to the company commander.

292. The noncommissioned officer in charge of quarters receives his orders from the company commander.

293. He will instruct the room orderly or orderlies in their duties.

294. He will be responsible for the proper police of the company quarters, rears, bath-rooms, amusement-rooms, barber and tailor shops, and the yard or vicinity of barracks.

295. He will have charge of company fatigue details and direct them in their work of policing.

296. Where the company is quartered in more than one squad-room, he will not be held responsible for the police of the squad-rooms unless so directed by the company commander.

297. He will report promptly to the company commander any necessary repairs of the barracks, barrack furniture, quartermaster or company property which may come under his observation.

298. He will see that all lamps are filled, cleaned, and trimmed during the day for lighting at night.

299. He will promptly quell all disturbances and disorderly or noisy conduct in the barracks or vicinity, and will report the same to the first sergeant.

300.   He is responsible during his tour for the proper care of all company property or Government property in possession of the company, and will not permit it to be damaged, or removed without proper authority.   The first sergeant or quartermaster-sergeant of the company is authorized to remove such property in their discretion.

301.   He will be excused from all other duty unless otherwise directed by proper authority.

302.   He will hold himself in readiness to accompany the company commander on his daily inspection of the company quarters, and will see that all directions of the company commander are promptly complied with.

303.   In camp his duties will include all those heretofore prescribed and such others as may be prescribed by competent authority.

CHAPTER XII.

THE SERGEANT OF THE GUARD.

304.   The senior noncommissioned officer of the guard always acts as sergeant of the guard, and, if there be no officer of the guard, will perform the duties prescribed for the commander of the guard.

305.   At guard mounting the sergeant of the guard remains in his place in the file-closers in rear of the company detail until the command: 1. *Noncommissioned officers, front and center,* 2. *March.* Then he executes the right shoulder arms, passes around the nearest flank of the guard, along the front, and takes place on the right of the line of noncommissioned officers, three paces in rear of the officer of the guard; or, if there be no officer of the guard, three paces in front of the adjutant.   At the command: 1. *Noncommissioned officers,* 2. *Posts,* 3. *March,* he faces about and takes the post of chief of the first platoon, as prescribed in the school of the company. If there be no officer of the guard, the noncommissioned officer commanding the guard takes post on the right of the right guide, when the guard is in line; and takes post of the officer commanding the guard, when in column or passing in view.

306.   If there be no officer of the guard, the sergeant of the guard commands the guard while passing in review, and will bring the guard to the eyes right when at a point about six paces from the officer of the day and will salute with the rifle salute when at six paces from the officer of the day, remaining at the salute until the guard has passed six paces beyond the reviewing officer.   Having passed the reviewing officer, he will form the guard into column of squads without halting and march it to the guard-house or other designated post.   If there be no division of platoons, and if there be present an officer of the guard, the sergeant of the guard takes post in the line of file-closers in rear of the right squad of the guard.

307. Having arrived at the post of the guard, the new guard marches in quick time past the old guard, the sergeant of the guard, if in command, saluting with the rifle salute.

308. As the new guard approaches the guard-house, the old guard is formed in line, with its field music three paces to its right; and, when the field music at the head of the new guard arrives opposite its left, the commander of the new guard commands: 1. *Eyes*, 2. *Right;* the commander of the old guard commands: 1. *Present,* 2. *Arms;* commanders of both guards salute. The new guard marches in quick time past the old guard.

When the commander of the new guard is opposite the field music of the old guard, he commands: *Front;* the commander of the old guard commands: 1. *Order,* 2. *Arms.*

The field music, having marched three paces beyond the field music of the old guard, changes direction to the right, and, followed by the guard, changes direction to the left, when on a line with the old guard; the changes of direction are without command. The commander of the guard halts on the line of the front rank of the old .guard, allows his guard to march past him, and, when its rear approaches, forms it in line to the left, establishes the left guide three paces to the right of the field music of the old guard, and on a line with the front rank, and then dresses his guard to the left; the field music of the new guard is three paces to the right of its front rank.

309. The new guard being dressed, the commander of each guard, in front of and facing its center, commands: 1. *Present,* 2. *Arms*, resumes his front, salutes, carries saber, faces his guard, and commands: 1. *Order,* 2. *Arms.*

Should a guard be commanded by a noncommissioned officer, he stands on the right or left of the front rank, according as he commands the old or new guard, and executes the rifle salute.

310. The detachments and sentinels of the old guard are relieved and, as they come in, form on its left; the commander of the old guard then marches it, with the guide right, six paces to the

front, then in column of squads to the right; the field music begins to play and the guard marches in quick time past the new guard, both guards saluting.

311. Upon arriving on the parade-ground, the commander of the old guard forms it in line, opens and closes chamber, orders successively the company details two paces to the front, and sends each, under charge of a noncommissioned officer, or private, to its company.

312. To receive prisoners at the guard-house after their number has been verified by the officer of the day, the sergeant of the guard forms his guard with an interval in the middle of it sufficient for the prisoners when in line and in double rank, and commands: 1. *Prisoners,* 2. *Right face,* 3. *Forward,* 4. *March.* The prisoners having arrived opposite the interval in the new guard, he commands: 1. *Prisoners,* 2. *Halt,* 3. *Left face,* 4. *Right* (or *left*) *backward dress,* 5. *Front.* The prisoners dress on the line of the new guard.

313. After the salutes have been acknowledged by the officers of the day, each guard is brought to the order by its commander; the commander of the new guard then directs the orderly or orderlies to fall out and report. and causes bayonets to be fixed if so ordered by the commanding officer. He then falls out members of the guard for detached posts, placing them under charge of the proper noncommissioned officers, divides the guard into three reliefs, first, second, and third from right to left.

314. The sergeant of the guard has general supervision over the other noncommissioned officers and the musicians and privates of the guard, and must be thoroughly familiar with all their orders and duties.

315. He is directly responsible for the property under charge of the guard and will see that it is properly cared for. He will make lists of articles taken out by working parties and will see that all such articles are duly returned. If not, he will immediately report

the fact to the commander of the guard or, if there be none, to the officer of the day.

316.   Immediately after guard mounting he will prepare duplicate lists of the names of all noncommissioned officers, musicians, and privates of the guard, showing the relief and post or duties of each.   One list will be handed as soon as possible to the commander of the guard; the other will be retained by the sergeant of the guard.

317.   He will see that reliefs are turned out on time and that the corporals thoroughly understand and are prompt and efficient in the discharge of their duties.

318.   During the temporary absence from the guard-house of the sergeant of the guard, the next in rank of the noncommissioned officers present will perform his duties.

319.   Should the corporal whose relief is on post be called away from the guard-house, the sergeant of the guard will designate a noncommissioned officer to take his place until his return.

320.   After breakfast, he will cause the guard-house or guard-tent and the space around it to be policed by the prisoners if there be any, or by the members of the guard if there be no prisoners.

321.   He will see that the guard-room and cells are thoroughly policed twice daily, morning and evening.

322.   At first sergeant's call he will proceed to the adjutant's office and obtain the guard report book.

323.   The absence of the color-bearer and guard, when the national or regimental colors are taken from the stacks of the color line, the sergeant of the guard unarmed, and two privates of the guard armed, will escort the colors to the Colonel's quarters as prescribed in the Infantry Drill Regulations.

324.   Upon the return of soldiers having passes, the passes will be given to the sergeant of the guard, who will endorse upon it the time at which each of the men included in a pass returns; at guard mounting he will turn them in to the commander of the guard.

325.   He will report to the commander of the guard any sus-

picious or unusual occurrence that comes under his notice, will warn him of the approach of any armed body, and will send to him all persons arrested by the guard.

326. When the guard is turned out the formation will be as follows: The senior noncommissioned officer, if commander of the guard, is on the right of the right guide; if not the commander, he is in the line of file-closers, in rear of the right squad of the guard; the next in rank is right guide; the next left guide; the others in line of file-closers, usually each in rear of his relief; the field music, with its left three paces to the right of the right guide. The reliefs form in the same order as when the guard was first divided, except that if the guard consists of dismounted cavalry and infantry, the cavalry forms on the left.

327. The sergeant forms the guard, calls the roll, and, if not in command of the guard, reports to the commander of the guard in the manner prescribed for the first sergeant forming a troop or company; the guard is not formed into platoons or sections, and except when the whole guard is formed prior to marching off, they do not count off.

328. The sergeant reports as follows: *"Sir, the guard is present"*; or, *"Sir, the guard and prisoners are present"*; or, *"Sir, the guard is present and the prisoners are secured"*; or, *"Sir, (So-and-so) is absent"*; or, if the roll call has been omitted, *"Sir, the guard is formed."* Only men absent without authority are reported absent. He then takes his place without command.

329. At night the roll call may be by reliefs and numbers instead of names; thus, the first relief being on post: "Second relief, Corporal; No. 1, No. 2, etc. Third relief, Corporal, etc."

330. Calling the roll will be dispensed with forming the guard when it is turned out as a compliment, on the approach of an armed body, or in sudden emergency; but in such cases the roll may be called before dismissing the guard. If the guard be turned out for an officer entitled to inspect it, the roll will, unless he directs otherwise, always be called before a report is made.

331.   When directed by the officer of the guard to dismiss the guard, the sergeant salutes, steps in front of the guard, and commands: 1. *Port*, 2. *Arms*, 3. *Open chamber*, 4. *Close chamber*, 5. *Dismissed;* or, 5. *Order*, 6. *Arms*, 7. *Stack*, 8. *Arms*, 9. *Dismissed.*

332.   The sergeant of the guard has direct charge of the prisoners and is responsible to the commander of the guard for their security.

333.   He will carry the keys of the guard-room and cells and will not suffer them to leave his personal possession while he is at the guard-house, except as hereinafter provided.   Should he leave the guard-house for any purpose, he will turn the keys over to the noncommissioned officer who takes his place.

334.   He will count the knives, forks, etc., given to the prisoners with their food, and see that none of these articles remain in their possession.   He will see that no forbidden articles of any kind are conveyed to the prisoners.

335.   Prisoners, when paraded with the guard, are placed in the line in its center.   The sergeant, immediately before forming the guard, will turn over his keys to the noncommissioned officer at the guard-house.   Having formed his guard, he will divide it into two nearly equal parts.   Indicating the division with his hand, he commands: 1. *Right*, 2. *Face*, 3. *Forward*, 4. *March*, 5. *Guard*, 6. *Halt*, 7. *Left*, 8. *Face*.   If the first command be *Right face*, the right half of the guard only will execute the movements; if *Left face*, the left half only will execute them.   The command *Halt* is given when sufficient interval is obtained to admit the prisoners.   The doors of the guard-room and cells are then opened by the noncommissioned officer having the keys.   The prisoners will then file out under the supervision of the sergeant, the noncommissioned officer and the sentinel on duty at the guard-house, and such other sentinels as may be necessary; they will form in line in the interval between the two parts of the guard.

336.   To return the prisoners to the guard-room and cells, the

sergeant commands: 1. *Prisoners,* 2. *Right,* 3. *Face,* 4. *Forward,* 5. *Column right,* 6. *March.* The prisoners, under the same supervision as before, return to their cells.

337. To close the guard, the sergeant commands: 1. *Left* (or *right*), 2. *Face,* 3. *Forward,* 4. *March,* 5. *Guard,* 6. *Halt,* 7. *Right* (or *left*), 8. *Face.* The left or right half only of the guard, as indicated, executes the movement.

338. If there be but few prisoners, the sergeant may indicate the point of division as above, and form the necessary interval by the command: 1. *Right* (or *left*) *step,* 2. *March,* 3. *Guard,* 4. *Halt,* and close the interval by the same commands.

339. If the sentinels are numerous, reliefs may, at the discretion of the commanding officer, be posted in detachments, and sergeants, as well as corporals, required to relieve and post them.

340. Sergeants assigned to reliefs perform the duties prescribed for corporals of the guard. They will not be so assigned unless the number of corporals detailed for guard be less than the number of reliefs.

341. If the sergeant of the guard be also the commander of the guard, he will, in addition to what has already been prescribed, be governed by the following instructions for the commander of the guard.

342. The commander of the guard is responsible for the instruction and discipline of the guard. He will see that all its members are correctly instructed in their orders and duties, and that they understand and properly perform them.

343. He receives and obeys the orders of the commanding officer and of the officer of the day, and reports to the latter without delay all orders not given or transmitted by him; he transmits to his successor all material instructions and information relating to his duties.

344. He is responsible under the officer of the day for the general safety of the post or camp as soon as the old guard marches

away from the guard-house. In case of emergency occurring while both guards are at the guard-house, the senior commander of the two guards will be responsible that the proper action is taken.

345. Except in emergencies, he may divide the night with the next in command, but retains his responsibility; the one on watch must be constantly on the alert.

346. When any alarm is raised in the camp or garrison, the guard will be formed immediately. If the case be serious, the proper call will be sounded, and the commander of the guard will cause the commanding officer and the officer of the day to be at once notified.

347. If the sentinel calls: "The guard," the commander of the guard will at once send a patrol to such sentinel's post. If the danger be great, in which case the sentinel will discharge his piece, the patrol will be as strong as possible.

348. When practicable, there should always be at least one noncommissioned officer and two privates at the guard-house, in addition to the sentinel there on post.

349. The commander of the guard will see that the guard is formed promptly, and under arms, whenever it is turned out for any purpose whatever.

350. When a guard commanded by a noncommissioned officer is turned out as a compliment or for inspection, the noncommissioned officer, standing at the right shoulder on the right of the right guide, commands: 1. *Present,* 2. *Arms.* He then himself executes the rifle salute. If a report is required, he will, after saluting and before bringing his guard to an order, report as prescribed for the report of the sergeant of the guard to the officer of the guard.

351. Between retreat and reveille, the commander of the guard salutes and reports, but does not bring the guard to a present.

352. To those entitled to have the guard turned out, but not entitled to inspect it, no report will be made; nor will a report be made to any officer unless he halts in front of the guard.

353. A noncommissioned officer marching a guard or relief will salute all officers.

354. A guard being in line and not under inspection, when commanded by a noncommissioned officer, is brought to attention when an officer not entitled to have the guard turned out passes, and the noncommissioned officer salutes with the rifle salute.

355. If a person entitled to compliment pass in rear of the guard, it does not salute, but stands at an order, facing to the front.

356. After a person entitled to the compliment has been saluted by the guard or guards, official recognition of his presence thereafter, while he remains in the same vicinity, will be taken by bringing the guard or guards to attention.

357. The commander of the guard will inspect his guard at retreat and reveille to assure himself that the men are in proper condition to perform their duties and that their arms and equipments are in proper order; for inspection by other officers, he prepares the guard for inspection as directed in each case by the inspecting officer.

358. Any person having authority to inspect the guard, and who wishes to do so, will, after its commander has reported, direct him to prepare it for inspection, stating in what manner.

359. The guard will not be paraded during ceremonies unless so directed by the commanding officer.

360. At all formations of the guards or reliefs, he will see that the chambers and magazines of all rifles or carbines are opened as soon as the men have fallen in.

361. After receiving the report of the corporal, he will inspect each relief before it goes on post to assure himself that every sentinel is properly armed and equipped and is in proper condition to perform his duties. The same rule applies to all patrols and sentinels over prisoners. The relief first posted after guard mounting need not be thus inspected.

362. He will see that sentinels are habitually relieved every two hours, unless the weather or other cause make it necessary or proper that it be done at shorter or longer intervals, as directed by the commanding officer.

363. He will question the noncommissioned officers and sentinels as to instructions they may have received from the old guard; he will see that patrols and visits of inspection are made as directed by the officer of the day.

364. He will see that the orders for each sentinel are posted, either written or printed, in the guard-house, and, if practicable, in the sentry-box or other sheltered place to which the sentinel has constant access.

365. He will see that the proper calls are sounded as directed by the commanding officer.

366. Should a member of the guard be taken sick, or be arrested, or desert, or leave his guard, the commander of the guard will at once notify the adjutant.

367. He will, when the countersign is used, communicate it to the noncommissioned officers of the guard and see that it is duly communicated to the sentinels before the hour for challenging; the countersign will not be given to the sentinels posted at the guard-house.

368. He will have the details for hoisting the flag at reveille, and lowering it at retreat, made in time for the proper performance of these duties. He will see that the flags are kept in the best condition possible, and that they are never handled except in the proper performance of duty.

369. The commander of the guard may permit the members of the guard, while at the guard-house, to remove their headdress, overcoats, and gloves; if they leave the guard-house for any purpose whatever, he will require them to be properly equipped and armed according to the character of the service in which they are engaged, or as directed by the commanding officer.

370. He will enter in the guard report a report of his tour of duty, and on the completion of the tour, will present it to the officer

of the day. He will transmit with his report all passes turned in at the post of the guard.

371. Whenever a prisoner is sent to the guard-house or guard-tent for confinement, the commander of the guard will cause him to be searched, and will, without unnecessary delay, report the case to the officer of the day.

372. If any one is to be passed out of the camp at night, he will be sent to the commander of the guard, who will have him passed beyond the line of sentinels.

373. The commander of the guard will detain at the guard-house all suspicious characters, or parties attempting to pass a sentinel's post without proper authority, reporting his action to the officer of the day, to whom persons so arrested will be sent, if necessary.

374. He will inspect the guard-room and cells, and the irons of such prisoners as may be ironed, at least once during his tour and at such other times as he may deem necessary.

375. He will see that the sentences of prisoners under his charge are executed strictly as confirmed by the reviewing authority.

376. He will cause sentinels over working parties to be taken from those assigned to posts guarded at night only. If there be none, he will cause this duty to be divided as equally as possible among the privates of the guard.

377. He will inspect all meals sent to the guard-house for prisoners, and see that the quantity and quality are in accordance with regulations.

378. At guard mounting he will report to the old officer of the day all cases of prisoners whose terms of sentence expire on that day, as also all cases of prisoners concerning whom no statement of charges has been received.

379. While both guards are at the post of the guard, and after

each has been presented to its officer of the day, if other persons entitled to the salute approach, each commander of the guard will bring his guard to attention if not already at attention. The senior commander of the two guards will then command: 1. *Old and new guards*, 2. *Present*, 3. *Arms*. The junior will present at the command *Present arms*, given by the senior. After the salute has been acknowledged, the senior brings both guards to the order.

CHAPTER XIII.

THE CORPORAL OF THE GUARD.

380. Corporals of the guard are assigned to reliefs by the com-mander of the guard. They are assigned to reliefs according to rank, the senior corporal having command of the first relief, etc.

381. The corporal of the guard receives and obeys orders from none but noncommissioned officers of the guard senior to himself, the officers of the guard, the officer of the day, and the commanding officer.

382. It is the duty of the corporal of the guard to post and relieve sentinels, and to instruct the members of his relief in their orders and duties.

383. Immediately after the division of the guard into reliefs the corporals will assign the members of their respective reliefs to posts by number, and a soldier so assigned to a post will not be changed to another during the same tour of guard duty, unless by the direction of the commander of the guard or higher authority.

Usually, experienced soldiers are placed over the arms of the guard and at remote and responsible posts.

384. Each corporal will then make a list of the members of his relief, including himself. This list will contain the number of the relief, the name of the company, the regiment of every member thereof, and the post to which each is assigned. The list will be made in duplicate, one list to be given to the sergeant of the guard as soon as completed, the other to be retained by the corporal.

385. As soon as directed by the officer of the guard, the corporal of the first relief posts his relief.

386. The corporal forms his relief and then commands: *Call off*. Commencing on the right, the men call off alternately, rear and front rank, "one," "two," "three," and so on; if in single rank, they

Formation of Relief
marching on Post

New Corp

Old Corp

$\longrightarrow$

Formation for relieving
a Sentinel.

Relief   6 paces   New Sentinel   Old Sentinel

New Corp:

Old Corp

call off from right to left. The corporal then commands: 1. *Right*, 2. *Face*, 3. *Forward*, 4. *March.* If formed in single rank, the corporal commands: 1. *Twos right*, 2. *March.* In wet weather the relief may be marched at secure arms.

387. The corporal marches on the left and near the rear file, in order to observe the march. The corporal of the old guard marches on the right of the leading file, and takes command when the last one of the old sentinels is relieved, changing places with the corporal of the new guard.

388. When a relief arrives at six paces from a sentinel, the corporal halts it and commands, according to the post: *No.* (———). At this time the old sentinel should be standing in the middle of his beat, facing the relief and at the right shoulder. Both sentinels execute port arms or saber; the new sentinel approaches the old, halting at about one pace from him.

389. The corporals advance and place themselves, facing each other, a little in advance of the new sentinel, the old corporal on his right, the new corporal on his left, both at the right shoulder, and observe that the old sentinel transmits correctly his instructions. (See diagram on opposite page.)

390. The instructions relative to the post having been communicated, the new corporal commands, *Post.* Both sentinels then resume the right shoulder, face toward the new corporal, and step back so as to allow the relief to pass in front of them. The new corporal then commands: 1. *Forward*, 2. *March.* The old sentinel then takes his place in rear of the relief as it passes him, his piece in the same position as those of the relief. The new sentinel stands fast at a right shoulder until the relief has passed six paces beyond him, when he walks his post. The corporals take their posts as the relief passes them.

391. The sentinels at the guard-house are the first relieved; they are left at the guard-house. All others will march with the relief.

392. On the return of the old relief, the new corporal falls out

when the relief halts; the corporal of the old guard forms his relief on the left of the old guard, salutes, reports to the commander of the guard: *"Sir, the relief is present"*; or, *"Sir, (So-and-so) is absent,"* and takes his place in the guard.

393.   To post a relief after the sentinels of the old guard have been relieved, the corporal forms it by the commands: 1. *(Such) relief,* 2. *Fall in;* and, if the arms are stacked, 3. *Take,* 4. *Arms.* The relief is formed in double rank, facing to the front with arms at an order; the men place themselves according to the numbers of their respective posts—*viz.,* the even numbers in the front rank, the odd numbers in the rear rank, numbers one and two being on the right. The corporal, standing about two paces in front of the center of the relief, commands: 1. *Call,* 2. *Off.* The men call off as heretofore prescribed. The corporal then commands: 1. *Port,* 2. *Arms,* 3. *Open chamber,* 4. *Close chamber,* 5. *Order,* 6. *Arms;* faces the commander of the guard, salutes with the rifle salute, reports, *"Sir, the relief is present"*; or, *"Sir, (So-and-so) is absent,"* and then takes his place on the right at the order arms.

394.   Having inspected the relief, the commander of the guard directs the corporal, *Post your relief.* The corporal salutes and posts his relief as prescribed for the first relief. The corporal of the relief on post does not go with the new relief unless it be necessary to show the way.

395.   If so directed by the commander of the guard, the corporal, before posting his relief, will command: 1. *With ball cartridges,* 2. *Load,* 3. *Lock,* 4. *Pieces,* 5. *Order,* 6. *Arms.*

396.   To dismiss the old relief, it is halted and faced to the front at the guard-house by the corporal of the new relief, who then falls out; the corporal of the old relief steps in front of the relief, and commands: 1. *Port,* 2. *Arms,* 3. *Open chamber,* 4. *Close chamber,* 5. *Dismissed;* or, 5. *Order,* 6. *Arms,* 7. *Stack,* 8. *Arms,* 9. *Dismissed.*

397.   Should the pieces have been loaded before the relief was

posted, the corporal will, before dismissing the relief, see that no cartridges are left in the chambers or magazines. The same rule applies to sentinels over prisoners.

398. Each corporal will thoroughly acquaint himself with all the special orders of every sentinel on his relief, and see that each sentinel correctly transmits such orders in detail to his successor.

399. He will see that each sentinel, on being posted, clearly understands the limits and extent of his post.

400. There should be at least one noncommissioned officer constantly on the alert at the guard-house—usually the corporal whose relief is on post. This noncommissioned officer takes post near the entrance to the guard-house, and does not fall in with the guard when it is formed. He will have his rifle with him constantly.

401. Whenever it becomes necessary for the corporal to leave his post near the entrance to the guard-house, he will notify the sergeant of the guard, who will at once take his place, or designate another noncommissioned officer to do so.

402. He will see that no person enters the guard-house or guard-tent or crosses the post of the sentinels there posted without proper authority.

403. Should any sentinel call for the corporal of the guard, the corporal will, in every case, at once and quickly proceed to such sentinel. He will notify the sergeant of the guard before leaving the guard-house.

404. He will at once report to the commander of the guard any violation of regulations or any unusual occurrence which is reported to him by a sentinel, or which comes to his notice in any other way.

405. Should a sentinel call, "The Guard," the corporal will promptly notify the commander of the guard.

406. Should a sentinel call, "Relief," the corporal will at once proceed to the post of such sentinel, taking with him the man next for duty on that post. If the sentinel is relieved for a short time

only, the corporal will again post him as soon as the necessity for his relief ceases.

407. When the countersign is used, the corporal at the posting of the relief during whose tour the challenging is to begin gives the countersign to the members of the relief, excepting those posted at the guard-house.

408. He will, at the proper time, notify No. 1 of the hour, if the sentinels are required to call the hours or half-hours of the night.

409. He will wake the corporal whose relief is next on post in time for the latter to verify the prisoners, form his relief, and post it at the proper hour.

410. Should the guard be turned out, each corporal will call his own relief and cause its members to fall in promptly.

411. Tents or bunks in the same vicinity will be designated for the reliefs, so that all members of each relief may, if necessary, be found and turned out by the corporal in the least time and with the least confusion.

412. When challenged by a sentinel, while posting his relief, the corporal commands: 1. *Relief,* 2. *Halt.* To the sentinel's challenge he answers, "Relief," and at the order of the sentinel, he advances alone to give the countersign, or to be recognized. When the sentinel says, "Advance, Relief," the corporal commands: 1. *Forward,* 2. *March.* If to be relieved, the sentinel is then relieved as prescribed.

413. Between retreat and reveille, the corporal of the guard will challenge all suspicious-looking persons or parties he may observe, first halting his patrol or relief, if either be with him. He will advance them in the same manner that sentinels on post advance like parties; but if the route of the patrol be on the line of a continuous chain of sentinels, he should not challenge persons coming near him unless he has reason to believe that they have eluded the vigilance of the sentinels.

414. Between retreat and reveille, whenever so ordered by an

officer entitled to inspect the guard, the corporal will call, *Turn out the guard*, announcing the title of the officer, and then, if not otherwise ordered, he will salute and return to his post.

415. Between retreat and reveille, on the approach of an armed party other than a relief or other detachment of the guard, he will call, *Turn out the guard, armed party*, and remain where he can observe the movements of the party while the guard is forming, and then return to his post.

416. As a general rule, he will advance parties approaching the post of the guard in the same manner that sentinels advance like parties.. Thus the sentinel at the guard-house challenges and repeats the answer to the corporal; the corporal, advancing at a port arms, says, *Advance, (So-and-so), with the countersign*, or *to be recognized*, if there be no countersign used; the countersign being correctly given, or the party being duly recognized, the corporal says, *Advance, (So-and-So)*, repeating the answer to the challenge of the sentinel.

417. When officers of different rank approach the guard-house from different directions at the same time, the senior will be advanced first, and will not be made to wait for his junior.

418. Out of ranks and under arms, the corporal salutes with the rifle salute. He will salute all officers, whether by day or night. If marching his relief, he will bring his relief to *eyes right* before saluting the commanding officer and his superiors.

419. The corporal examines parties halted and detained by sentinels, and if he have reason to believe that the parties have no authority to cross sentinels' posts, will conduct them to the commander of the guard.

420. The corporal of the guard will arrest all suspicious-looking persons prowling about the post or camp, all persons of disorderly character disturbing the peace, and all persons taken in the act of committing crime against the Government on a military reservation or post. All persons arrested by corporals of the guard, or by sen-

tinels, will be at once conducted to the commander of the guard by the corporal.

421.   When the guard detail falls in on the company parade-ground, the corporals fall in in the line of file-closers.   They retain this position after the formation of the guard and until the command: 1. *Open*, 2. *Rank*, when they step three paces to the rear and dress to the right.

422.   At the command by the adjutant: 1. *Officer and non-commissioned officers, front and center*, 2. *March*, the noncommissioned officers execute the right shoulder, pass by the nearest flank, and, moving along the front, form in order of rank, from right to left, three paces in rear of the officer; if there be no officer of the guard, they form in line three paces in front of the adjutant.   They remain at the right shoulder.   At the command: 1. *Noncommissioned officers*, 2. *Posts*, 3. *March*, they face about and take the posts assigned them, as prescribed in the School of the Company, with open ranks, and order arms.

423.   The morning and evening gun will be fired by a detachment of the guard consisting, when practicable, of a corporal and two privates.   The morning gun is fired at the first note of the reveille, or, if the marches be played before the reveille, it is fired at the commencement of the first march.   The retreat gun is fired at the last note of retreat.   The corporal marches the detachment to and from the piece, and the piece is fired, sponged out, and secured under his direction.

CHAPTER XIV.

THE REGIMENTAL SERGEANT-MAJOR.

1. The regimental sergeant-major is the principal assistant to the regimental adjutant. He will, preferably, be selected from the noncommissioned officers of the regiment who are most distinguished for efficiency, bravery, and soldierly bearing. Paragraph 251, A. R. 1908.

2. He is the senior noncommissioned officer of the regiment. In the clerk's office at regimental headquarters, he is the representative of the adjutant, and his orders should be obeyed without question.

3. At *first sergeant's call*, he will transmit all routine orders and communications to the first sergeants, either by posting them on the bulletin-board or verbally. He will assist the first sergeants, especially those of recent appointment, with information and advice as to the proper preparation of returns, reports, letters, etc.

4. Under no circumstances, except by permission of the adjutant, will he give out any information concerning the administration of the regiment, or of any other matters passing through his office. He should not gossip about official matters, either in or out of the office.

5. He will not lend communications, books, maps, etc., pertaining to Headquarters, to anyone, except by permission of the adjutant.

6. He is responsible, under the adjutant, for the proper care and preservation of all regimental, noncommissioned staff, and band records. He will supervise the clerks at regimental headquarters in the work pertaining to the regimental, noncommissioned staff, and band records; he will see that files of all orders, circulars, letters, retained copies of rolls, returns, etc., are properly kept.

He will see that copies of Army Regulations at Headquarters are amended to date, and he should be required to keep a memorandum-book of records of events pertaining to the regiment for the information of the adjutant in compiling the regimental history.

7.   He is responsible to the adjutant for all Government and regimental property at headquarters.

8.   He will see that the janitor at headquarters keeps the rooms and lavatories clean and orderly. He will also see that the headquarters is kept properly heated and lighted.

9.   If the regiment has a printing press, he will, under the adjutant, be in immediate charge of the enlisted men employed in the printing office.

10.   He is charged with the duty of keeping all rosters pertaining to the noncommissioned officers and musicians and of personally making all details for guard, fatigue, and other duties.

11.   In the field, in addition to his clerical duties, he should assist the adjutant in keeping the records of field orders, messages, etc., received and sent, carefully noting the time of receipt and dispatch of orders, messages, etc.

In the field, the regimental sergeant-major should be mounted, else he will be of little use to either adjutant or commanding officer.

12.   In all formations of the regiment in line, the regimental noncommissioned staff officers, the sergeant-major on the right, form, at one pace apart, on the right of the noncommissioned staff of the first battalion; in column, the interval between them is such that they cover the head of the column. Paragraph 350, I. D. R.

13.   In the formation of the regiment, the regimental noncommissioned staff takes post as the last battalion is being formed on the line. Paragraph 352, I. D. R. When the last battalion is nearing the line, the regimental sergeant-major forms the regimental noncommissioned staff in line, with one pace interval, the left about thirty paces in rear and one pace to the right of the noncommissioned staff of the first battalion. He gives the command: 1. *Draw,*

2. *Saber;* followed by: 1. *Forward,* 2. *Guide left,* 3. *March.* He halts the noncommissioned staff one pace in rear of the line, each taking the order saber upon halting, and dresses it to the left without leaving his place in line.

At regimental review, at the command of the Colonel: 1. *Prepare for review,* 2. *Open ranks,* the regimental noncommissioned staff officers carry saber. At the command: 3. *March,* they are dressed to the left, the line verified by the sergeant-major, who then gives the command *Front,* at which command they turn their heads and eyes to the front and take the order saber.

14. In passing in review, the regimental sergeant-major gives to the noncommissioned staff the same commands for changing direction and for saluting the reviewing officer as are given to the company by the company commander. He should previously caution the noncommissioned staff to extend its front during the second change of direction to cover the head of the column—*i. e.,* the front of the leading company.

15. At regimental inspection, on the approach of the inspector, the adjutant gives the command: 1. *Inspection,* 2. *Arms.* At the second command, the noncommissioned staff officers take the carry saber. When the inspector approaches each, each executes the first motion of the present saber, turning the wrist to show both sides of the blade when the inspector is in front of him and resuming the carry saber when the inspector has passed. As soon as inspected, the noncommissioned staff may be dismissed. The adjutant gives the commands: 1. *Return,* 2. *Saber,* 3. *Noncommissioned staff and color guard,* 4. *Dismissed.*

At inspection with field equipment, after the inspection above described, the adjutant should give the necessary commands for returning sabers, after which he would give the necessary commands for unslinging and inspection of packs, remaking of packs, dismissal, etc.

16. At muster, as the mustering officer approaches, the adjutant

brings the noncommissioned staff to the carry saber, if not already there, and commands: 1. *Attention to muster.* The mustering officer or the adjutant then calls the roll; and as each man's name is called, he answers, "Here," and takes the order saber. Paragraph 399, I. D. R.

17. There is nothing prescribed in Infantry Drill Regulations as to the post of the regimental sergeant-major in extended order. It is believed that he, with the rest of the noncommissioned staff, should take post in rear of the Colonel and his staff.

18. At *adjutant's call*, the adjutant, dismounted, and the sergeant-major on his left, march to the parade-ground. The adjutant halts and takes post so as to be twelve paces in front of and facing the center of the guard when formed; the sergeant-major continues on, moves by the left flank, and takes post facing to the left, twelve paces to the left of the front rank of the band; the band plays in quick or double time; the details are marched to the parade-ground by the first sergeants; the detail that arrives first is so marched that, upon halting, the breast of the right front-rank man shall be near to and opposite the left arm of the sergeant-major; the first sergeant halts his detail, places himself in front of and facing the sergeant-major, at a distance equal to or a little greater than the front of his detail, and commands: 1. *Right*, 2. *Dress.* The detail dresses up to the line of the sergeant-major and first sergeant, the right front-rank man placing his breast against the left arm of the sergeant-major; the noncommissioned officers take post two paces, and the supernumeraries nine paces, in rear of the rear rank of the detail. The detail aligned, the first sergeant commands: *Front*, salutes, and then reports: "*The detail is correct*"; or, "(*So many) sergeants, corporals*, or *privates are absent*"; the sergeant-major returns the salute with the right hand after the report is made; the first sergeant then passes by the right of the guard and takes post three paces in rear of his supernumerary.

Each of the other details is formed in like manner on the left of the one preceding; the privates, noncommissioned officers, supernumerary, and the first sergeants .of each detail dress on those of the preceding details in the same rank or line; each first sergeant closes the rear rank to the right and fills in blank files, as far as practicable, with men from his front rank.

The company details alternate in taking the right of the line. Paragraph 508, I. D. R.

When the last detail has been formed, the sergeant-major takes a side step to the right, draws sword, verifies the detail (passing down the front of the guard, around the left flank, and in rear of the guard to his post), takes post two paces to the right and two paces in front of the guard, facing to the left, causes the guard to count off, completes the left squad, if necessary, as in the school of the company, and if there be more than three squads, divides the guard into two platoons (leaving his post to indicate the point of division, if necessary), again takes post as described above, and commands: 1. *Open ranks,* 2. *March.*

At the command *March,* the rear rank steps back and halts three paces in rear of the front rank; the noncommissioned officers three paces in rear of the rear rank; all dress to the rank. The sergeant-major verifies the alignment of the ranks, file-closers, supernumeraries, and first sergeants, again takes post as described above, and commands, *Front,* moves parallel to the front rank until opposite the center, turns to the right, halts midway to the adjutant, salutes, and reports: *"Sir, the details are correct";* or, *"Sir, (so many) sergeants, corporals,* or *privates are absent";* the adjutant returns the salute, .directs the sergeant-major: *Take your post,* and then draws saber; the sergeant-major faces about, approaches to within two paces of the center of the front rank, turns to the right, moves three paces beyond the left of the front rank, turns to the left, halts on the line of the front rank, faces about, and brings his sword to the order. Paragraph 509, I. D. R.

During inspection of the guard, if the adjutant approaches him, the sergeant-major executes *inspection saber.*

When the guard is presented to the new officer of the day, he salutes as prescribed.   Paragraph 526, I. D. R.

When the guard has been presented to the new officer of the day and has been formed in column of platoons to the right, the sergeant-major places himself six paces from, and abreast of, the front rank of the second platoon.

If the guard be not divided into platoons, the sergeant-major takes post abreast of the front rank, covering the adjutant.

If the march in review is omitted and the guard is marched to its post in column of squads or twos, the sergeant-major, remaining in place, returns sword with the adjutant, salutes the adjutant with the right hand, and retires.

When marching in review, the sergeant-major salutes with the adjutant.

Having passed twelve paces beyond the officer of the day, the adjutant halts; the sergeant-major halts abreast of the adjutant and one pace to his left; they then return saber, salute, and retire.

19.   In camp, the tents of the noncommissioned staff and band are at the head of the column.   Paragraph 563, I. D. R.

The sergeant-major's tent is on the flank of the line toward the officer's line.

20.   The sergeant-major is not required, but is permitted, to attend the annual target practice of the command.

He is required to take the dismounted course in pistol practice.

He is entitled to the extra pay provided by law for qualification at target practice.

21.   The sergeant-major is allowed one room as quarters.   For heating allowance, he is given the fuel prescribed in A. R. 1044.

He is allowed the illuminating supplies prescribed in A. R. 1057. The allowances for heat and light are cumulative during any fiscal year, provided that at no time the accumulated allowance be exceeded.

The allowance for subsistence is that prescribed for all enlisted men.

The clothing allowance is determined by the length of his service.

22. When traveling under orders without troops, the sergeant-major is entitled to a double berth in a sleeping-car, or to the customary stateroom accommodations on steamers, where extra charge is made for the same. A. R. 1136.

23. The allowance of baggage of a sergeant-major to be transported at public expense on a permanent change of station is 3,000 pounds. This allowance is in excess of the weights transported free of charge under the regular fare by public carriers. A. R. 1136.

24. On board any Army transport, the sergeant-major is subsisted at the ship's officer's mess. He will be assigned by the transport quartermaster to a second-class cabin or dormitory quarters, according to rank, when such accommodations and quarters are available.

25. The arms and equipments of a sergeant-major, as prescribed in G. O. No. 23, War Department, 1906, are as follows:

1 noncommissioned officer's sword;
1 waist-belt for garrison service;
1 frog;
1 revolver;
1 revolver holster;
1 revolver cartridge box for garrison service;
1 revolver cartridge belt, with fasteners;
1 first aid package, with pouch for same;
1 canteen, haversack, meat can, cup, knife, fork, and spoon;
1 set blanket-roll straps;
2 canteen-haversack straps;
1 shelter tent half;
1 shelter tent pole;
5 shelter tent pins.

CHAPTER XV.

THE CHIEF MUSICIAN, THE PRINCIPAL MUSICIAN.

The Chief Musician.

1.   The duties of the chief musician are nowhere clearly and distinctly defined, but depend upon the will of the commanding officer of the band. In some bands, he is charged with the administrative and disciplinary duties of a first sergeant of a company. In this case, his duties in general will be those prescribed for the first sergeant as prescribed in Chapter IX., as far as they may pertain to the band, with the exception of the clerical work, which is usually performed in the adjutant's office under the supervision of the sergeant-major. In some regiments, he is charged only with the musical instruction of the band, together with the discipline of the band as far as it pertains to that instruction. In such cases, the administrative and disciplinary duties of the first sergeant are imposed upon the drum-major.

2.   In general, however, he should be in direct charge of the band during all formations, rehearsals, concerts, or other musical duties required of it.

3.   He is responsible for the musical instruction of the band. Ordinarily it will devolve upon him to select proper music, assign members of the band to instruments, give instructions for individual practice, and, in every way, to be responsible for the musical efficiency of the band.

4.   He is the senior noncommissioned officer of the band, and should receive his orders and instructions direct from the commanding officer and the adjutant.

5.   He should make recommendations to the adjutant in regard to the appointment and promotions of noncommissioned officers of the band.

6. He should supervise the drum-major and principal musician in the performance of their duties.

The Principal Musician.

1. He should assist the chief musician in the musical instruction of the band, take his place in case of sickness or absence, and should be in charge of and responsible for the instruction of the field musicians.

CHAPTER XVI.

THE DRUM-MAJOR.

1. When so ordered, the drum-major's duties in the discipline and administration of the band are similar to those prescribed for the first sergeant in Chapter IX.

2. He is generally charged with the duties of mess sergeant as prescribed in Chapter X., and with the property responsibility prescribed for the quartermaster-sergeant in the same chapter.

3. Unless living apart from barracks, he is responsible for the order and police of the same at all times. '

4. He should accompany the adjutant at daily inspections of the quarters.

5. At military formations of the band he has charge of and marches it. He should thoroughly acquaint himself with the post of the band at all formations for the battalion and the regiment at all ceremonies.

6. The post of the drum-major is three paces in front of the center of the band. He gives the signals or commands for the movements of the band as for a squad, substituting in the commands *band* for *squad*. Paragraph 536, I. D. R.

7. With the battalion in line, the band is posted with the left of its front rank twenty-four paces to the right of the front rank of the battalion.

In column, it marches with its rear rank twenty-four paces in front of the leading company, or its front rank twenty-four paces in rear of the rear company, according to the direction in which the battalion is facing. In the line of columns, the band retains its line position, marching abreast of the leading guides.

The field music, if present within the band, forms in rear of it.

8. For the formation of the battalion, and before *adjutant's call*

s sounded, the band takes a position designated by the adjutant at
a signal from him, the drum-major causes the band to sound the
adjutant's call. When the call has been sounded, he causes the
band to play a march and marches it at the same time as the companies to its position on the line. Paragraph 262, I. D. R.

9. At formations of the regiment in line, in line of columns, and
in line of masses, the band is posted with the left of its front rank
twenty-four paces to the right of the first battalion. In evolutions,
it takes, as far as practicable, the positions prescribed in the School
of the Battalion, unless excused or a position is assigned to it by the
Colonel. Paragraph 334, I. D. R.

10. At the formation of the regiment, the movements of the
band are the same as prescribed in paragraph 8, except that *adju-
ant's call* is sounded twice, once for the formation of the battalions
and, the second time, for the formation of the regiment. After the
second sounding of the call, the band plays a march and moves to
its place in the formation.

11. At reviews, the band of each regiment plays while the
reviewing officer is passing in front of and in rear of the regiment.

Each band, immediately after passing the reviewing officer, turns
out of the column, takes post in front of him, continues to play
until its regiment has passed, then ceases playing and follows in
rear of its regiment; the band of the following regiment commences
to play as soon as the preceding band has ceased.

When marching in review, but one band in each brigade plays
at a time, and but one band at a time when within one hundred
yards of the reviewing officer.

12. In line, when the color salutes, the march, flourishes, or
ruffles are sounded by all the field music; in passing in review, by
the field music with the band that is halted in front of the reviewing
officer, the band continuing to play.

13. At battalion review, while the reviewing officer is going
round the battalion, the band plays, ceasing when he leaves the
right to return directly to his post. Paragraph 717, I. D. R.

When passing in review, the drum-major causes the band to change direction at the indicated points without command from the officer commanding the review.

14.   The drum-major salutes and executes *Front,* when passing in review, at the same points prescribed for the Major.   Paragraph 725, I. D. R.

15.   The band ceases to play when the column has completed its second change of direction after passing the reviewing officer. Paragraph 725, I. D. R.

16.   If the batalion is marched in review in double time, the band plays in double time.   Paragraph 725, I. D. R.

While playing in double time, it remains in its position in front of the reviewing officer, commencing to play at the command: 1. *Double time,* 2. *March.*

The review terminates when the last company has passed the reviewing officer (in double time); the band then ceases to play and, unless otherwise directed by the Major, returns to the position occupied before marching in review, or is dismissed.   Paragraph 726, I. D. R.

At regimental review, in passing in review, the band marches with its rear rank thirty-six paces in front of the leading company. Paragraph 728, I. D. R.

17.   At battalion parade, at the command *Sound off,* from the adjutant, the band, playing in quick time, passes in front of the captains to the left of the line and back to its post on the right, when it ceases playing.   At evening parade, when the band ceases playing, *retreat* is sounded by the field music, and following the last note, and while the flag is being lowered, the band plays "The Star-Spangled Banner."   Paragraph 734, I. D. R.

18.   The officers having closed and faced to the front, the senior company officer commands: 1. *Forward,* 2. *Guide center,* 3. *March.* The officers advance, the band playing. . . . It continues to

play while they march to the front, salute, and return to their posts. . . . The music ceases when all officers have resumed their posts.

After marching in review, the band continues to play while the companies are in march upon the parade-ground. Paragraph 734, I. D. R.

Should the officers not return to their posts with their companies, the band ceases to play as they move to take post with the staff of the Major. Paragraph 734, I. D. R.

19. At regimental parade, the band, playing in quick time, passes in front of the adjutant and field officers to the left of the regiment and back to its post on the right, when it ceases playing. Paragraph 734, I. D. R. During the parade, it plays as prescribed for the parade of the battalion.

20. At battalion inspection, at the command: 1. *Prepare for inspection,* 2. *March,* the drum-major conducts the band, if not already there, to its position in rear of the column, and opens ranks. Paragraph 734, I. D. R.

The adjutant gives the necessary commands for the inspection of the band. Paragraph 735, I. D. R.

The band plays during the inspection of the companies. Paragraph 735, I. D. R.

When the inspector approaches the band, the adjutant commands: 1. *Inspection,* 2. *Instruments.* As the inspector approaches him, each man raises his instrument in front of the body, reverses it so as to show both sides, then returns it to its former position.

21. In escorting the color: The escort is formed in column of platoons, the band in front; the escort then marches without music to the Colonel's quarters or office, and is formed in line, facing the entrance, the band on the right.

When the escort presents arms to the colors, the field music sounds *to the color.*

When the colors have been received, the escort is formed in

column of platoons and marches in quick time back to the regiment, the band playing; the march is so conducted that when the escort arrives at fifty paces in front of the right of the regiment, the direction of its march shall be parallel to its front.

While arms are being presented to the color in front of the regiment, the field music again sounds *to the color.*

When the escort is marching back to its post, after presenting the colors to the regiment, the band plays until the escort has passed the left of the line, when it ceases playing and returns to its post on the right, passing in rear of the regiment. Paragraph 736, I. D. R.

22. In the funeral escort, the escort is formed opposite the quarters of the deceased, the band on the flank of the escort toward which it is to march.

Upon the appearance of the coffin, the commander commands: 1. *Present*, 2. *Arms*, and the band plays an appropriate air.

The escort marches slowly, to solemn music.

While the coffin is being carried along the front of the escort to the grave, the bands play an appropriate air. The coffin having been placed over the grave, the music ceases.

When the ceremony has been completed, the escort is formed in column and marched in quick time to the point where it was assembled and dismissed. The band does not play until it has left the enclosure. Paragraph 739, I. D. R.

23. When the distance to the place of interment is considerable, the escort, after having left the camp or garrison, may march *at ease* in quick time until it approaches the burial-ground. The band does not play while marching *at ease.* While marching at *attention*, the field music may alternate with the band in playing. Paragraph 739, I. D. R.

24. The field music sounds the marches, flourishes, or ruffles, according to the rank of the deceased, whenever arms are presented, after which the band plays an appropriate air. Paragraph 739, I. D. R.

25. At guard mounting: The band takes post on the parade, so that the left of its front rank shall be twelve paces to the right of the front rank of the guard when the latter is formed.

At a signal from the adjutant, *adjutant's call* is sounded, after which the band plays in quick or double time as directed, continuing to play until the last detail of the guard has been halted upon the line.

During the inspection the band plays. A concert selection is usually played at this time. During the rendering of this selection, the chief musician usually takes his post in front of the band to lead it, and the drum-major retires to the file-closers until the selection has been finished.

When the guard has been brought to *parade rest*, the band, playing, passes in front of the officer of the guard to the left of the line and back to its post on the right, when it ceases playing.

When column is formed to march in review, the band turns to the right and places itself with its rear rank twelve paces in front of the first platoon.

The march in review is conducted on the same principles as for review, the band turning out of column and continuing to play until the guard has marched off the parade-ground.

26. The band is formed in two or more ranks with sufficient intervals between the men and distances between the ranks to permit a free use of the instruments.

When a battalion or regiment turns about by squads, the band executes the countermarch; when the battalion or regiment executes *right, left,* or *about face,* the band faces in the same manner.

In marching, the different ranks dress to the right.

In executing *open ranks,* each rank takes the distance of three paces from the rank next in front; the druum-major verifies the alignment.

The field music sounds the *march, flourishes,* or *ruffles,* and *to the color* at the signal of the drum-major.

27.   The signals of the drum-major: Preparatory to a signal, the staff is held in the right hand, hand below the chin, back to the front, head of the staff near the hand, ferrule pointing upward and to the right.

Prepare to play: Face toward the band and extend the right arm to its full length in the direction of the staff.   *Play:*   Bring the arm back to its original position in front of the body.

Prepare to cease playing: Extend the right arm to its full length in the direction of the staff.   *Cease playing:*   Bring the arm back to its original position in front of the body.

To march: Turn the wrist and bring the staff to the front, the ferrule pointing upward and to the front; extend the arm its full length in the direction of the staff

To halt: Lower the staff into the raised hand and raise the staff horizontally above the head with both hands, the arms extended; lower the staff with both arms to a horizontal position at the height of the hips.

To countermarch: Face toward the band and give the signal to *march.*   The countermarch is executed by each front-rank man to the right of the drum-major turning to the right about, each to the left turning to the left about, each followed by the men covering him.   The drum-major passes through the center.

To oblique: Bring the staff to a horizontal position, the head of the staff opposite the neck, the ferrule pointing in the direction the oblique is to be made; extend the arm to its full length in the direction of the staff.

To march by the right flank: Extend the arm to the right, the staff vertical, ferrule upward, back of the hand to the rear.

To march by the left flank: Extend the arm to the left, the staff vertical, ferrule upward, back of the hand to the front.

To diminish front: Let the ferrule fall into the left hand at the height of the eyes, right hand at the height of the hip.

To increase front: Let the ferrule fall into the left hand at the height of the hip, right hand at the height of the neck.

The march, flourishes, or ruffles: Bring the staff to a vertical position, hand opposite the neck, back of hand to the front, ferrule pointing down.

To the color. Bring the staff to the horizontal position at the height of the neck, back of hand to the rear, ferrule pointing to the left.

When the band is playing in marching, the drum-major beats the time with his staff and supports the left hand at the hip, fingers in front, thumb to the rear.

The drum-major, before making his report at parade, salutes by bringing his staff to a vertical position, head of the staff up and opposite the left shoulder.

The drum-major, marching in review, passes the staff between the right arm and the body, head of the staff to the front, and then salutes with the left hand.

At a halt, the band not playing, the drum-major holds his staff with the ferrule touching the ground about one inch from the toe of the right foot, at an angle of about sixty degrees, ball pointing upward to the right, right hand grasping the staff near the ball, back of the hand to the front; the left hand at the hips, fingers to the front, thumb to the rear. Paragraph 781, I. D. R.

28. The drum-major is responsible for the marching of the band, and may drill it in all marching movements until it is proficient.

CHAPTER XVII.

THE COLOR SERGEANTS.

1. The color sergeants are regimental noncommissioned staff officers. They are selected from among the noncommissioned officers of the regiment who have the longest and most honorable service. They bear the colors at all formations where the colors are present, and are charged with the safe-keeping and preservation of them at all times.

2. The color guard consists of the two color sergeants, who are the color-bearers, and two experienced men selected by the Colonel. The senior color sergeant carries the National Color; the junior color sergeant carries the Regimental Color. The Regimental Color, when paraded, is always on the left of the National Color, in whatever direction the battalion faces.

The colors are kept at the office or quarters of the Colonel, and are escorted thereto and therefrom by the color guard, which is formed and marched in one rank, the color-bearers in the center Paragraph 767, I. D. R.

3. The color guard, by command of the senior color sergeant, presents arms on receiving and parting with the colors. After parting with the colors, the color guard is brought to the order arms by the command of the senior member, placed as the right man of the guard. Paragraph 775, I. D. R.

4. At drills and ceremonies, excepting escort of the color, the color, if present, is received by the color company after its formation. The word *color* implies the National Color and includes the Regimental Color when both are present.

The formation of the color company completed, the captain faces to the front; the color guard, conducted by the senior sergeant, approaches from the front and halts at a distance of ten paces from the captain, who then faces about, brings the company to the present, faces to the front, salutes, again faces about and brings the company to the order, the color guard comes to the present and order at the command of the captain, and is then marched by the color sergeant directly to its post on the left of the color company. Paragraph 776, I. D. R.

5. The color company is the left company of the right wing (of the battalion); the color guard remains with it unless otherwise directed.

In line, the color is between the inner guides of the right and left wings; the members of the guard in the line of file-closers in rear of the color.

In line of columns, the color guard, in one rank, is midway between the wings and on line with the captains.

In column of companies, platoons, or sections, the color guard, in one rank, is midway between the wings and equidistant from the flanks of the column.

In column of squads, the color is between the wings, abreast of the guide of the color company, in front or in rear of the file or files next to the file-closers; the other members of the guard retain their places in the line of file-closers.

If, by movements of the battalion, the color guard finds itself not between the wings, it takes post there as soon as practicable. Paragraph 772, I. D. R.

6. The color, when with a battalion that takes the battle formation, joins the regimental reserve, whose commander either directs the color to join a certain company or detaches a guard to remain with it during the action.

7. When ranks are opened, the color-bearers remain in place; the other members of the color guard step back with the file-closers. Paragraph 772, I. D. R.

8. If the company or battalion is faced about by the command: 1. *About,* 2. *Face,* the color-bearer steps into the rear, now become he front rank. Paragraph 772, I. D. R.

9. When the colors and the guard halt in front of the color company, the colors are brought to the order and remain there while arms are being presented.   Paragraph 771, I. D. R.

10. At reviews, when the rank of the reviewing officer entitles him to the honor, each color salutes at the command *Present arms*, given or repeated by the Major of the battalion with which it is posted; and again in passing in review.

11. In the Escort of the Color, when the escort has been formed in column of platoons, the color-bearer takes the post midway between the platoons, equidistant from the flanks; when the line is formed in front of the Colonel's office or quarters, the color-bearer takes post in the line of file-closers.

The color-bearer, preceded by the first lieutenant and followed by a sergeant of the escort, then goes to receive the color.   .

He enters the building, secures the color, comes out, and halts facing the escort. When arms have been presented, *the color* sounded, and the escort formed in column of platoons, the color-bearer takes post between the platoons as before. When line is formed in front of the regiment, the color-bearer, passing between the platoons, advances and halts twelve paces in front of the Colonel. He executes the color salute at the command, *Present arms*, of the Colonel. The Colonel then faces about and brings the regiment to the order, at which the color-bearer resumes the carry and takes his post with the color company.

12. At funeral escorts, when the rank of the deceased is such as to have entitled him to the honor, the color salutes whenever arms are presented.

13. At the *carry*, the heel of the pike rests in the socket of the sling at the right hip; the right hand grasps the pike at the height of the right shoulder.

At the *order*, the heel of the pike rests on the ground near the right toe, the right hand holding the pike in a vertical position.

At *parade rest*, the heel of the pike is on the ground, as at the order; the pike is held with both hands in front of the center of the body, left hand uppermost.

The order is resumed at the command *Attention*.

The *carry* is the habitual position when the troops are at the shoulder, port, or trail.

The *order* and *parade rest* are executed with the troops.

The *color salute:* Being at the carry, slip the right hand up the pike to the height of the eye, then lower the pike by straightening the arm to the front.

The color salutes in the ceremony of the Escort of the Color, and when saluting an officer entitled to the honor, but in no other case.

If marching, the salute is executed when at six paces from the officer entitled to the salute; the carry is resumed when at six paces beyond him.

At a halt, the salute is executed at the command *Present arms*, the color being brought to the carry at the command *Present;* the salute executed, the order is resumed at the command *Order arms*, the color being first brought to the carry. Paragraph 778, I. D. R.

14. The officers below named are entitled to the salute by the color: The President, the General, the Lieutenant-General, a Major-General, a Brigadier-General, the Vice-President, Members of the Cabinet, the Chief Justice, the President of the Senate, the Speaker of the House of Representatives, American or Foreign Ambassadors, Governors within their respective States and Territories, the Assistant Secretary of War, American or Foreign Envoys or Ministers, Officers of the Navy of the assimilated rank of Brigadier-General or higher, Officers of Marines, Volunteers, and Militia, when in the service of the United States when of the rank of Brigadier-General or higher, and to officers of foreign sevices if of the rank of Brigadier-General or higher. Paragraph 375, A. R.

15.   On the march, the colors are ordinarily carried cased.   In camp, during fair weather, the colors are displayed in front of the tent of the Colonel, flying free from *reveille* to *retreat*.   At *retreat*, they are cased and removed to the Colonel's tent.

The color sergeants are charged with the duty of attending to this.

CHAPTER XVIII.

The Provost Sergeant.

1. The provost or police sergeant is the assistant to the police officer of the post or camp. He is usually selected from among the noncommissioned officers of the regiment on account of his energy, trustworthiness, and known ability to control and direct the labor of men.

2. Under the police officer, he is in direct charge of the work of all prisoners at the post. He is also in charge of the work of all general and special fatigue parties, and is held responsible for the proper police of the post or camp.

3. At a designated hour each day, generally after recall from fatigue, he reports to the police officer for instructions as to the work for the following day. At the same time, he makes report concerning the progress of police or other work under way.

4. At *fatigue call* he is present at the guard-house and assigns the prisoners, under proper guard, to tasks of general and special police work. He also takes charge of the fatigue parties and assigns them to work.

5. During the day he visits all working parties frequently, to see that they are working according to instructions and that they do not shirk. He also makes inspection after the completion of work to see that it has been properly done.

6. He may be placed in charge of the delivery of fuel and illuminating supplies.

7. On board transport, under the police officer, he has charge of the various police details and will supervise the police of all parts of the ship occupied by troops, especially the parts used in common, such as baths, latrines, and wash-rooms. He will see that troop

decks are swept clean each morning, and the mess decks after each meal.

8. In a post or camp of any considerable size, the provost sergeant is usually furnished a mount.

CHAPTER XIX.

REGIMENTAL COMMISSARY SERGEANT.

1. The regimental commissary sergeant is a member of the regimental noncommissioned staff. He is selected by the regimental commander, preferably from noncommissioned officers of the regiment who are most distinguished for efficiency, excellence of character, gallantry, and soldierly bearing. He is usually assigned to duty in the subsistence department at the post where the regiment is serving, or he may be assigned to such other duties, not inconsistent with his rank and position, as the regimental commander may order.

2. In the field he assists the regimental commissary in making issues and in caring for the property for which the regimental commissary may become responsible.

3. He should have a thorough knowledge of all the papers pertaining to the subsistence department, so that he is able to assist the commissary in preparing returns, reports, etc., required to be rendered.

4. He should be familiar with the care and preservation of subsistence stores and property—that is, how stores are arranged in the store-room and the method of caring for same. This being a very important part of his duties, he should carefully study all details pertaining thereto. He should be a good store-keeper as well as a clerk, and always bear in mind that troops depend upon the commissary for susbsistence, especially in the field.

LIST OF REPORTS, RETURNS, ETC., RENDERED BY THE COMMISSARY.

Account Current: Form 1, is a report of all public funds for which the commissary has been accountable during the period covered. It is supported by numerous other forms, showing expenditures and receipts.   It is forwarded to the Commissary-General not later than the 10th of each month.

Return of Subsistence Stores: Form 19, is a consolidated statement of all stores for which the commissary was accountable during the period covered.   It is forwarded to the Commissary-General not later than the 10th of each month.

Return of Subsistence Property: Form 30, is a form similar to the return of subsistence stores.   It covers a period of six months ending June 30th and December 31st.   It is forwarded to the Commissary-General not later than July 10th and January 10th.

Requisition for Subsistence Stores and Funds: Form 41, is one of the important papers rendered by the commissary.   The period for which stores and funds are called for is designated by the chief commissary of the department; the amounts usually called for being based on previous consumption for same period.   On this form is also entered the amount of stores on hand at the end of each month, and the amount received, shipped, gained, saved, and condemned during the month, and the amount consumed during the past period for which the requisitions call for.   From the commissary book the consumption of the various articles is readily figured and used as a basis for the monthly requisition.   The requisition is submitted to the post commander for approval on the first day of each month, and should be forwarded to the chief commissary on the same day.

Requisition for Subsistence Property: Form 30, is for authorized articles of subsistence property and will be made out, semi-annually, on January 1st and July 1st, for periods of twelve months, and mailed, after approval of the post commander, to the chief commissary, not later than the 15th of the month in which made.   A careful inventory of all property on hand will be taken before the requisition is made.

Requisition for Blanks: Form 44, is for blank forms to be used by commissaries.   In the United States, at posts, arsenals, and in the field, this requsition is forwarded to the Commissary-General;

in the Philippines, to the Chief Commissary of the Division.   Such requisitions should be made ordinarily for a seven-months supply for a garrisoned post, beginning June 1st and December 1st, and should be mailed direct.

Office Records Consist of the Following: Correspondence book, a document file, order file, a sales book, cash book, commissary book, inventory book, and such memorandum books as may be found necessary.

CHAPTER XX.

REGIMENTAL QUARTERMASTER SERGEANT.

1. The regimental quartermaster sergeant is appointed by the regimental commander on the recommendation of the regimental quartermaster. The appointment is generally made from the older noncommissioned officers, the selection being made from those conversant with the papers of the Quartermaster's Department and the care of property, and is also a reward for faithful service.

2. He assists the quartermaster in preparing estimates, requisitions, reports, returns, and other papers pertaining to the department, and in receiving, shipping, and issuing property. If there is a post quartermaster sergeant stationed at the post, these duties are divided, each taking charge of some special part of the work.

3. He should familiarize himself with Army Regulations and current orders, especially those that pertain to the Quartermaster's Department and to money and property accountability; also with the circulars issued from time to time from the office of the Quartermaster-General.

MONEY ACCOUNTS.

4. Money accounts are rendered monthly, direct to the Quartermaster-General, and should be mailed by the 10th of the ensuing month.

The principal money papers are as follows:

Form No. 6, Account Current___ This f o r m, with its various vouchers, should show all funds received and disbursed for the period rendered.

Form No. 26, Invoice of Funds___ Used in all transfers of funds. No receipt is given unless the transfer is in cash.

Form No. 25, Abstract C_____ For convenience, all funds transferred to officers on Form 26 are entered on this form, and totals only under each appropriation are carried to the account current. With slight alterations in the headings, this form is also used when necessary for funds received from officers.

Form No. 7, Abstract of Funds received from sales to officers.

Form No. 45, Account of Sales at Auction_____ Used only when sales of condemned quartermaster's supplies are made by order of an inspector.

Form No. 8, Abstract of Purchases_____ For convenience, all vouchers for purchases are entered on this form under the several appropriations, and totals only are carried to the account current.

Form No. 10, Voucher for Purchases_____ This form is used for all purchases, except for articles for which a special form is provided. It is the only purchase voucher ordinarily used by post quartermasters.

Forms 31, 31a, and 31b, Report of of Purchases_____ On these forms, assembled, all articles purchased during the month are entered in alphabetical order, and all items purchased are carried to the return of quartermaster's supplies.

Form No. 11, Abstract of Ex-
penditures------------------ For convenience, all vouchers
for expenditures are entered on
this form under the several appropriations, and totals only are
carried to the account current.
The principal vouchers entered on Form 11 are:
Form No. 12, Receipt Roll -----   This form is generally used when
more than one permanent em-
ployee is paid from any appropriation. Separate rolls should
be made for civilian employees
and extra duty men, and distinct
g r o u p s under the several item
numbers of each appropriation.
Form No. 13, Individual Voucher
for Services---------------- This form is used for temporary
services, either personal or non-
personal, and may be used for
permanent employees when only
one person is paid from a certain
appropriation or when payment
is made for only a part of a month.
All payments made on the above vouchers (12 and 13), either personal or non-personal, are reported
to the Quartermaster-General on
Form No. 1. An original and duplicate are prepared at the commencement of services, and the
original transmitted with the first
account current. The duplicate
is retained, all payments made are
noted thereon, and when the ser-

vice is completed or the employee is relieved, discharged, or for any other reason leaves the service, it is forwarded with the first account current. In cases where the service commences and terminates in the same month, both copies are transmitted as above.

Funds received from sales to officers or at auction are placed in a designated depository, to the credit of the Treasurer of the United States, under the several appropriations. A duplicate certificate of deposit is received, which is filed with the retained papers.

Form No. 28, Estimate of Funds__ This form is used in estimating for all funds required for payment for supplies purchased and is submitted whenever necessary.

Form No. 146, Request for Funds
for Services_ _ _ _ _ _ _ _ _ _ _ _ _ _ _ _ This form is used in asking for all funds required for payment for services, either personal or nonpersonal. For payment of permanent employees it is submitted on the first of the month for such funds as are required. For other expenses it is submitted when required.

RETURN OF QUARTERMASTER'S SUPPLIES.

This form, No. 27 (front cover), 27a (original return), 27b (duplicate return), and 27c (back cover), when assembled, shows all property on hand at the beginning of the quarter, all property received, transferred, issued, and expended during the quarter, and on the bottom line all property remaining on hand at the close of the quarter. It is rendered quarterly, within twenty days after the close of the quarter. No abstracts are used, all vouchers being entered directly on the return.

Some of the principal vouchers are as follows:

Form No. 117, Combination Invoice and Receipt_____   This form is used in all transfers of property and is also used as a shipping invoice and receipt.

Form No. 65, Requisition for Clothing_____   Submitted by company commanders when clothing is required for issue to the men of their companics.

Form No. 38, Requisition for Fuel_____   Submitted monthly for expenditures for enlisted force at post.

Form No. 38a, Requisition for Forage, Straw, and Mineral Oil_____   Submitted monthly for expenditures for public animals and enlisted force at post.

Form 38d, Issues of Fuel,Forage, Straw, and Mineral Oil to Officers. Submitted monthly.

Form No. 41, Requisition for Stationery_____   Submitted quarterly for organizations and as required for other purposes.

Form No. 43, List of Q. M. Supplies Expended. Submitted monthly.

Supplies other than those purchased are received on estimates and requisitions, submitted generally at stated periods.

The principal estimates are:

Form No. 53, Estimate of Clothing_____ Submitted quarterly. On January 1st an estimate is submitted for the quarter ending June 30th. On April 1st an estimate is submitted for the quarter ending September 30th, etc. Care must be taken in compiling this estimate to prevent an accumulation of sizes of articles not often asked for.

Form No. 61, Estimate of Lamps, Lanterns, Oils, etc _____ Submitted quarterly, forty-five days before beginning of period for which supplies are needed.

Form No. 95, Estimate of Tableware and Kitchen Utensils____ Submitted quarterly, forty-five days before beginning of period for which supplies are needed. The number of each article allowed is fixed by general orders, and estimates are generally made to replace similar articles expended by organizations under their annual allowance for breakage, and those charged against enlisted men.

Form No. 60, Requisition_____   This form is used in estimating for all supplies for which a special form is not furnished. W h e n used as a quarterly requisition, it is submitted forty-five days before the period commences for which the supplies are required. It is also used as a special requisition when the exigencies of the service require supplies the need of which could not be foreseen when the quarterly estimates were prepared.

5.   In addition to the foregoing papers, there are numerous reports required at stated intervals, such as report of water supply, report of fire apparatus, report of progress of public buildings, report of typewriting machines, etc., and at posts where a Government boat is stationed, a monthly report of public service rendered, quarterly report of cost, etc.

6.   Bills of lading and transportation requests are issued as required.   Circular proposals for supplies or services, together with the necessary plans and specifications, are prepared when required.

7.   The principal books and records of the Quartermaster's Department are, a correspondence book, a cash book, record of interments, descriptive book of public buildings, descriptive lists of public animals, file of letters received, copies of all accounts, returns, and reports rendered, and of all estimates and requisitions submitted.

THIS BOOK IS DUE ON THE LAST DATE STAMPED BELOW

AN INITIAL FINE OF 25 CENTS

WILL BE ASSESSED FOR FAILURE TO RETURN THIS BOOK ON THE DATE DUE. THE PENALTY WILL INCREASE TO 50 CENTS ON THE FOURTH DAY AND TO $1.00 ON THE SEVENTH DAY OVERDUE.

JUN 10 1941

JUN 10 1941

CPSIA information can be obtained
at www.ICGtesting.com
Printed in the USA
BVHW04*1219210918
528171BV00010B/418/P